# WHO AM I?

## WHY AM I HERE?

*by Patricia Diane Cota-Robles*

**New Age Study of Humanity's Purpose**
**PO Box 41883**
**Tucson, Arizona 85717**
**USA**

**http://eraofpeace.org**

**Fax: 520-751-2981**
**Phone: 520-885-7909**

## DEDICATION

This book is dedicated to every awakening
Child of God who is seeking answers to the
age-old questions,
*"Who am I?"* and *"Why am I here?"*
The time for you to remember is NOW!

**Patricia Diane Cota-Robles**
**http://eraofpeace.org**

**Please visit this website for access to Patricia's**

**FREE Video Webinars**

**Weekly On-line Radio Program**
*"Awaken Your Divine Potential"*

**and additional**
**Books, CDs, and DVDs**

# TABLE OF CONTENTS

# INTRODUCTION

Humanity is in the midst of the greatest shift of consciousness we have ever experienced. This is causing an awakening to take place within the hearts and minds of men, women, and children all over the world. People are beginning to remember that they have a purpose and a reason for being on Earth at this particular time. They may not remember the specifics of their Earthly missions, but they are intensely motivated to find the answer to the questions that have piqued Humanity's curiosity from time immemorial. Those questions are *"Who am I?"* and *"Why am I here?"*

During our personal quests for understanding, we have all heard the words *"Ask and you shall receive"* and *"Knock and the door will be opened."* These statements are not just religious rhetoric; they denote a profound Truth. Whenever we sincerely ask for Divine Guidance, God and the Company of Heaven always respond. The response may come in unexpected ways, and sometimes we may not recognize the answer to our inquiry, but we always receive an answer.

Because of the awakening that is now taking place on Earth, there are literally millions of people sending forth the heartfelt plea for answers to the questions, *"Who am I?"* and *"Why am I here?"* In response to Humanity's sincere heartcalls, the floodgates of Heaven have opened. The Beings of Light in the Realms of Illumined Truth have been given permission to come through the veil to meet us halfway. God has granted a Cosmic Dispensation that allows the Company of Heaven unprecedented Divine Intervention into the lives of everyone on this planet. All we have to do is ask for their assistance.

It is difficult for us to fathom with our finite minds the magnitude of what this gift of Divine Grace truly means, but during this Cosmic Moment, Humanity is receiving more assistance from On High than ever before.

So who are these Beings of Light from the Realms of Illumined Truth? Who are these messengers of God who are willing to selflessly assist you and me and the rest of Humanity? They are our sisters and brothers. They are Sons and Daughters of God, just like you and me, but they are far more advanced in their evolutionary process.

These Children of God completed their lessons long ago in the 3rd-Dimensional schools of learning. They accomplished that facet of their Divine Plan either in this world or in another system of worlds where they learned to become cocreators with God. Upon graduation, they Ascended the Spiral of Evolution into the next dimension of their evolutionary process. They are now assisting all of us to do the same. These Beings of Light are the equivalent of college professors compared to you and me, who are the equivalent of kindergarten students.

In this book, these Beings will be interchangeably referred to as the Company of Heaven, the Legions of Light from the Realms of Illumined Truth, the Spiritual Hierarchy, and simply the Beings of Light. These illumined souls are also known in their various individual forms. There are Beings we call Saints, Ascended Masters, all of the graded orders of Angels, Solar Logos, Galactic Beings, Elohim, the Directors of the Elements, as well as all of the Beings we are familiar with who are associated with the various world religions such as Jesus, Krishna, Buddha, Moses, Mohammed, Saint Germain, Mother Mary, Kuan Yin, and every other known and unknown Being of Light throughout the whole of Creation.

These Beings abide in the 5th-Dimensional Realms of Illumined Truth and beyond. These are the multidimensional Realms of Light where the answers that Humanity is seeking are clearly present and easily obtained. These dimensions are what Humanity has always referred to as the Kingdom of Heaven.

The Heavenly Realms transcend the humanly created psychic-astral plane, which is a sea of negativity that surrounds this planet. The psychic-astral plane is an accumulation of Humanity's distorted thoughtforms, destructive behavior patterns, and erroneous belief systems. The Heavenly Realms cannot be contaminated or defiled by these human miscreations.

Within the Heavenly Realms, the Beings of Light serve as selfless messengers of our omniscient, omnipotent, omnipresent God—the Cosmic I AM—All That Is. They function from the highest levels of Integrity and Truth. They know that *we are One* and that all Life is interconnected, interdependent and interrelated. These Beings will assist us only in ways that are in alignment with our Divine Plans and the highest good for all concerned. They never interfere with our free will, and they intervene in our lives only if they are invited to do so.

Our Beloved Sisters and Brothers from the Realms of Truth are reminding us that there is a reason why Humanity is going through the unprecedented shift of consciousness we are now experiencing. The Earth and all Life evolving on this planet are in the midst of a unique experiment that has never been attempted in any system of worlds. The goal of this experiment is to awaken Humanity quickly, so that we will reverse the adverse effects of our fall from Grace in time to Ascend the Spiral of Evolution into the 5th Dimension with the rest of our Solar System. Never has a planet that has fallen this far into the frequencies of duality and separation been given the opportunity to Ascend through two dimensional shifts, from the 3rd to the 5th Dimension, in such a short period of time.

The Beings of Light have revealed that the reason for this unparalleled Ascension is that Humanity got into this mess out of the greatest act of Divine Love and Compassion ever demonstrated by the Sons and Daughters of God. Because of this fact, no one was willing to give up on us without giving us one final opportunity to change the direction in which we were headed.

The details of this facet of Earth's and Humanity's Divine Plans have been clearly described by the Company of Heaven. A condensed version of those details is contained within the pages of this book. This information may seem new to some of you, but it is not. Each and every person embodied on Earth at this time has been preparing for untold lifetimes to assist in this unique experiment. The Beings of Light are merely reminding us of what we have forgotten. We each have a unique thread of experience to weave into the Tapestry of Life on this planet, and no one else possesses the exact same thread. Every thread is vital and critical to the whole and to the fulfillment of this monumental unfolding Divine Plan.

Our God Selves have guided us through the exact learning experiences we needed to accomplish whatever it is we have volunteered to do in this lifetime. We are all in our right and perfect place, and our beliefs are sacred and important to our missions. The information being given to Humanity by the Beings of Light is not intended to dispute our present belief systems or to tell us that what we have accepted as Truth is wrong. The intent of these celestial sharings is to help us see the bigger picture and to give us greater clarity and understanding about the events occurring in our individual lives and on the planet. The goal is to help us put things into perspective and to empower us with knowledge, wisdom, encouragement, trust, and support during these wondrous but often challenging times.

God and the Company of Heaven do not want us ever to accept something as Truth just because someone told us it is true. They want us to take all information into the Flame of Illumined Truth pulsating in the deepest recesses of our hearts. Then we must ask our God Presence, the Divinity within our hearts, to reveal to us the Truth of the information and how it specifically applies to our individual Divine Plans.

The information being given to Humanity by the Company of Heaven during this auspicious moment is life transforming. Contained within these sacred Truths are the viable solutions to all of the maladies existing in both our individual and our collective lives. The Divine Intent of this book is not only to share this priceless information with you but to inspire you to go within to the Divinity of your own Heart Flame where you will directly access this sacred knowledge for yourself. It is far better for each of us to receive this information through our own God Presence. That way, we will not have these Truths interpreted for us through anyone else's perception.

Your God Presence has drawn this book into your sphere of awareness, because it is time for you to remember who you are and why you are on Earth at this time. As you peruse these pages, feel the Presence of God within you taking full dominion of your life. A new level of clarity and understanding is awakening within your heart and mind. From this moment forth, you will *"see with new eyes, and hear with new ears."*

And so it is.

# CHAPTER ONE

# A PERSONAL SHARING

The Beings of Light have revealed to Humanity that the greatest privilege and honor of any evolving soul, in any dimension, is physical embodiment on Planet Earth during this Cosmic Moment. That is because we are going through an experiment that has never been attempted in any system of worlds. If we succeed God Victoriously, we will create a new level of Godhood that will enhance the learning experiences of every Son and Daughter of God throughout the whole of Creation. This is why, for the first time ever, the entire Universe is focused on the progress of one tiny planet.

Earth's experiment is being carefully orchestrated through the unified efforts of the God Selves of every person on Earth and the entire Company of Heaven. Nothing is being left to chance, and we are receiving the maximum assistance from the Company of Heaven that Cosmic Law will allow.

In previous lifetimes, prior to embodiment, we would each be shown a panorama of the possible learning experiences we could go through, as well as the karmic liabilities for which we needed to make restitution. From that plethora of information, we would choose what we were willing to experience in our upcoming lifetime.

After the "Fall," we often chose the most challenging opportunities, so that we could clean up our past mistakes very quickly and move forward in the schoolroom of Earth at an accelerated pace. In making that decision we would say something like, *"I am going to take on as much as I can in this lifetime, so that I will learn my lessons quickly and clear up as much of my negative karma as possible. If I succeed, great. If I do not succeed, I will have another opportunity in a fu-*

*ture life to complete this learning experience."*

Now, everything has changed. The Earth and all her Life are dependent on the success of this experiment. In this lifetime no one, I repeat, *no one* has been allowed to volunteer to fulfill a facet of this Divine Plan that he or she has not already successfully accomplished in some other time frame or dimension. We do not have time to try again in a future lifetime. This is it! Our entire Solar System is waiting for the Earth to catch up, so that we can Ascend with them into the 5th Dimension. In this lifetime, the Earth and all her Life are hanging in the balance. If this experiment fails, we will be left behind. We *must* succeed.

The good news is that this means every single one of us has the ability to achieve whatever it is we volunteered to accomplish in this lifetime. No matter how colossal or complex the mission is that we volunteered for, we already have within us everything we need to succeed. This is true regardless of how inadequate or unprepared we may feel through the perception of our fragmented, fear-based human egos. The reality is, we have all of the strength, wisdom, knowledge, skill, courage, and willingness to be God Victorious. If that were not the case, we would not have been allowed to embody on Earth at this time.

Because of the need of the hour, each of us volunteered to be born into circumstances that would serve as a catalyst to help us awaken quickly. The catalysts we have chosen are probably as diverse as the people on the planet, but I would like to share with you a little about my personal experience. This is what catapulted me into my quest for answers as to why Humanity is experiencing so much pain and suffering, and what we can do about it. What I discovered has transformed my life and it will transform your life as well, because we are One. The Universal Law that applies to all of us clearly affirms, *"As I AM lifted up, all Life is lifted up with me."*

Prior to this embodiment, I volunteered to be born into a dysfunctional family. My father, bless his heart, was a very sick man. In this day and age, he would have been diagnosed with a bipolar disorder and there would have been treatments to help him cope with his mood swings. Unfortunately, in those days that option did not exist, so he self-medicated himself with copious amounts of alcohol. The only thing the doctors knew to do was to give him shock treatments, which only complicated the problem and made things much worse. When my father was in the euphoric stage of his disorder, he was very loving and affectionate. But without warning, he would plunge into a black depression, during which he became very violent and abusive.

My sister and I often found ourselves in situations that, from a child's perspective, seemed life-threatening. Amazingly, whenever I was in the midst of the violence, I had this knowing that somehow everything was going to be all right. I knew that I was going to survive the violence, and I understood that this was not the way people were supposed to treat each other. I remember my third birthday and things that happened before that time, so I would say that from the time I was two years old I had this inner knowing.

As I grew older, I was very sensitive to the pain and suffering people were experiencing and inflicting upon each other. I felt there had to be a better way, and I believed that if I searched for the answers I would find them. When I was in high school, I studied whatever I could find about the various world religions. No one I knew understood why people were being so mean to each other or why there was so much pain in the world, so I thought religions might have the answer.

When I got to the university, I explored things relating to Humanity's behavior. I studied psychology, sociology, and things involving the power of the mind and the laws of physics. After I left the university, I studied metaphysics and the sacred knowledge contained in the books associated with the various mystery schools.

Throughout my personal quest for answers, I became aware that there was a unifying thread that ran through all of the teachings with which I had come in contact. This thread of information kept presenting itself over and over again regardless of whether I was investigating religious teaching, scientific teachings, or metaphysical teachings. No matter where I looked, this principle, which is most commonly referred to as the *Law of the Circle,* kept seizing my attention.

In Eastern religions, this principle was referred to as the *"Law of Cause and Effect,"* or the *"Law of Karma."* In Judaism it was stated as, *"An eye for an eye or a tooth for a tooth."* The complete statement should have been, *"An eye for an eye, a tooth for a tooth, a hug for a hug, or a kiss for a kiss,"* so we would see the whole picture. In Christianity, this principle was reflected in the statements, *"We reap what we sow,"* and *"When we cast our bread upon the water, it returns to us."* In the field of science, the Law of the Circle was described as *"like attracts like,"* *"action and reaction,"* and *"radiation and magnetization."* Finally, when I studied metaphysics, this familiar principle was described as, *"the Outbreath and the Inbreath of God."*

In simple terms, the Law of the Circle dictates that what we send out through our thoughts, words, feelings, and actions must return to us. Therefore, at any given moment, our lives are reflecting the sum total of whatever it is that we have created through our past thoughts, words, feelings, and actions. Just contemplate that statement for a moment. *At any given moment, our lives are reflecting the sum total of whatever it is that we have created through our past thoughts, words, feelings, and actions.* This profound Truth applies to every man, woman, and child whether our behavior during our various Earthly sojourns was deliberate or inadvertent. How is that for an awesome responsibility?

With this realization it was clear to me that if we do not like what is happening in our lives, we have the ability to change things by improving the way we are thinking, speaking, feeling, and acting. This seemed like just plain common sense to me, a no-brainer. It was not rocket science. So my resounding question was, if all of the sources of information on this planet are confirming that through the Law of the Circle we have created our present realities, and that we have the ability to change the things that are taking place in our lives by improving our behavior—Why in the world is Humanity still in the mess we are in???

I began by seeking answers to that question from the religious leaders. They said, *"It is because Eve ate that darned apple. If Eve hadn't disobeyed God by eating that apple everything would be just fine."* Next, I went to the scientific community. Their response was, *"Matter evolves out of chaos by happenstance. Humanity evolved from an amoeba in a mud puddle by chance; there is no rhyme or reason for our existence. What is, just is."* Finally, I sought answers from the metaphysical community. I received more comprehensive explanations from that source, but there was still a lot of conflicting information. No one seemed to agree on the answer to the questions, *"Why doesn't Humanity understand this fundamental Law?"* *"Why do we just keep on perpetuating pain and suffering through our destructive behavior patterns?"*

Even though I was disappointed and somewhat dismayed by the explanations I received from the so-called knowledgable sources on the planet, I was not about to give up my quest for answers. I intuitively knew that there is order in the Universe and that God responds to our heartfelt pleas. So in the silence of my heart, I once again asked God for answers. After several days of quiet contemplation and listening, I clearly heard the words, *"Seek ye first the Kingdom of Heaven within, and all else will be given unto thee."*

These are words from the Bible that we have all heard, but what do they really mean? Well, we all know what Heaven is. Right? Heaven is the place we go after we die. This is where we meet Saint Peter. He greets us at the Pearly Gates, and if we have been good, he assigns us our Angel wings and gives us a golden harp. We then pass through the Pearly Gates and walk through streets of gold into a land of milk and honey. We find a white cloud to sit on, and we joyfully play our harp for the rest of eternity.

Truthfully, I could not imagine anything more boring than sitting on a white cloud playing a harp for eternity. I was convinced that was not the Kingdom of Heaven God was referring to in the words I was hearing. In deep humility and gratitude, I asked to be lifted into the very Heart of God for clarity and understanding. Shortly thereafter, I began to experience a deeper level of trust and a very calming inner peace.

Everyday I set aside some time to meditate, and to go within to the Divinity of my heart. This was the place I came to know through the mystery schools as the *Secret Place of the Most High Living God*. Within the sanctuary of my heart, I asked God to reveal to me the Kingdom of Heaven within. I patiently waited, trusting that in Divine Timing my prayers would be answered.

I do not remember just how long it took, but one day while I was meditating, I experienced a brilliant pinpoint of Light within my heart. As I focused my attention on this Light it began to slowly rotate and expand. Gradually, the pinpoint of Light became a spiraling Sun that enveloped my entire physical body. As I surrendered into the embrace of this resplendent Light, I was lifted up in energy, vibration, and consciousness. All of my senses were enhanced, and in a sublime moment of wondrous bliss, I felt that I had touched the Face of God.

When I returned from my meditation, I knew that the spiraling Sun of Light was now securely anchored within the Divinity of my heart. The next day when I went into my meditation, the pinpoint of Light in my heart was instantly present. I focused my attention on the Light, and it expanded into the spiraling Sun that enveloped my body in a matter of seconds. Once again, I was raised up in energy, vibration, and consciousness. I reveled in the wonder of what was happening to me, and I strove to consciously absorb whatever wisdom and knowledge God was revealing to me through this experience.

Day after day, the blissful joy of my meditations increased. Then one day in the midst of my meditation, I had an epiphany. In what seemed like a flash of enlightenment, I realized that what I was experiencing was perfectly normal. This was the way things were supposed to be for everyone. We were all supposed to have this very natural open-heart-and-mind telepathic communication with God. This was not about being psychic or channeling. This process was not supernatural, nor was I gifted in extrasensory perception. I was merely reclaiming the natural abilities that Humanity lost after our fall from Grace aeons ago. In that moment, I knew in the very core of my Being that open-heart-and-mind telepathic communication with God is Humanity's Divine Birthright. This was what was meant by a statement that had been reverberating in my heart over and over again during my meditations:

*"You are Sons and Daughters of God, and all that God has is yours."*

When I returned from my meditation that day, I was overwhelmed with gratitude and a sense of elation. I took a few minutes to assimilate my experience. Then in the embrace of complete surrender, the depths of which I had never experienced, I asked God what I could do to be the most effective force of God's Light on Earth. After a few moments, Beloved Jesus projected his luminous Presence into my mind's eye and said with overwhelming compassion:

*"Bring to the mankind of Earth the realization of their own Divinity."*

After an awestruck moment, I experienced a lucid reasoning and a level of insight that made Jesus' words crystal clear.

Of course! Humanity is cocreating this Earthly experience through our thoughts, words, feelings, and actions. We have all been programed by our fear-based human egos, and several manipulative outside sources, into believing that we are worthless sinners and worms in the dust. We become who we believe we are. As long as we keep empowering those lies, we will keep cocreating experiences that confirm that distorted belief system. It is impossible to fathom how dramatically things will change once Humanity remembers that each and every person is a Beloved Child of God, and that all God has is ours.

Even though I clearly understood what a monumental difference it will make when Humanity remembers who we are and why we are here, I was not sure how I could help with implementing this facet of the Divine Plan. I did know, however, that God and the Beings of Light in the Realms of Illumined Truth do not ever ask us to do something that we are incapable of accomplishing.

So once again, I called forth my deepest level of trust and invoked assistance from God. I attained a state of listening Grace and focused my attention on my inbreath and my outbreath. I asked and became One with the Holy Breath of God. After a period of time, I experienced a tangible shift within the Divinity of my heart. A new level of Divine Love and Compassion flooded through my Being. My perception was enhanced, and I was lifted up in consciousness. From that moment forth my meditations were transformed, and my open-heart-and-mind telepathic communication with the Beings of Light in the Realms of Illumined Truth expanded exponentially.

The next day, I sat down to meditate. As usual, I focused on the pinpoint of Light in my heart and watched as it expanded into a radiant Sun. This time, however, something was different. Instead of the Sun remaining as a spinning vortex of Light around me, it began to transform itself into a shaft of Light. While observing this metamorphosis, I realized that the shaft of Light was not just surrounding my physical body. It was extending into the Heavens as far as I could see, in my mind's eye.

As I watched in amazement, this shaft of Light Ascended through multidimensional Realms of Light into what I perceived to be the very Heart of God.

Suddenly, I became aware that this shaft of Light around me was simultaneously descending into the center of the planet, where it was securely anchored within the Divine Momentum pulsating in the heart of Mother Earth.

God revealed to me that this mighty shaft of Light, which now surrounded me and extended from the Heart of God into the center of the Earth, was an invincible forcefield of Divine Protection. God said this shaft of Light was being permanently established around me by my God Self and the Company of Heaven, so that I would be able to reach into the Realms of Illumined Truth without interference from the lower psychic-astral planes of illusion and chaos.

God affirmed that within this invincible forcefield of Divine Protection, I would be able to easily reach into the Realms of Illumined Truth to communicate with the Legions of Light throughout the whole of Creation. God reminded me that I would be able to seek out the answers to my questions, and that I would receive the information I needed in order to accomplish what Beloved Jesus had asked me to do.

There is a reason why I am sharing this very personal information with you. Please take the words of the following paragraph into the deepest recesses of your heart, and allow them to resonate in the Flame of Truth.

The experiences I have shared with you are not unique. I am not special, and my facet of the unfolding Divine Plan is not one iota more important than your facet of the Divine Plan. Humanity's ability to clearly communicate with our God Selves, God, and the Company of Heaven is our Divine Birthright. It is what God intended from the moment we were breathed forth from the core of Creation.

Tangible guidance from our more highly evolved sisters and brothers was intended to be a critical part of our learning experience on Earth. This profound Truth is beginning to awaken within the hearts and minds of people all over the world. Hopefully, by sharing my experiences you will realize that open-heart-and-mind telepathic communication with the Beings of Light is available to you, right here and right now. You do not have to take years to discover this wondrous opportunity. You just need to know that God is eagerly awaiting the opportunity to escort you into the Kingdom of Heaven within your heart where everything else will be revealed to you. All you have to do is ask.

An invincible forcefield of Divine Protection, which surrounds you, and extends from the Heart of God into the Divine Momentum in the center of Mother Earth, will be permanently created for you also. Just ask your God Self and the Company of Heaven for this precious gift of Light. Then perpetually feel this forcefield of Light around you. Know that no matter where you are or what you are doing in the process of fulfilling your Divine Plan, you are eternally protected.

It is time for you to fulfill your destiny. It is time for you to know and to accept the irrefutable Truth that YOU are a Beloved Child of God, and that ALL God has is yours.

Now, I would like to share with you what I have learned from the Beings of Light in the Realms of Illumined Truth. The Divine Intent of these celestial sharings is to inspire you to reach up in consciousness, so that you will tap into the Realms of Truth yourself. Then you will be able to confirm the reality of this sacred knowledge. You will learn how it specifically applies to you, and your Divine Plan, during the unprecedented experiment that Humanity and all Life evolving on this sweet Earth are now experiencing.

Please read this information with an open heart and an

open mind. Ask the Presence of God pulsating in your heart to reveal to you the Truth contained within these words. Focus on how this new perspective and this greater level of clarity might enhance your life and help you to accelerate the fulfillment of your Divine Plan.

Even though you may feel as though you are learning some of these things for the very first time, you are not. The information I am sharing in the pages of this book is already resonating in the Divinity of your heart. You are merely being reminded of what you have forgotten. This information is not new; it is why you volunteered to be on Earth during this Cosmic Moment. It is why you have been training for literally hundreds of lifetimes to learn how to fulfill your particular facet of the Divine Plan during this embodiment. The Truth contained in this book is designed to awaken within you the inner knowing that...

*"We are the ones we have been waiting for."*

This powerful statement was given to the world by the Native American tribe known as the Hopi.

# CHAPTER TWO

# ENTERING THE
# REALMS OF ILLUMINED TRUTH

Once the invincible forcefield of Divine Protection was securely established around me, I knew that I had the ability to safely Ascend into the Realms of Illumined Truth to communicate with the Beings of Light abiding there. I was not sure just how this would occur, but I knew a whole new level of opportunity was opening up for me.

I entered my meditative state, and I focused on the powerful shaft of Light that surrounded me. I asked my God Self to lift me into the Realms of Illumined Truth, and I patiently waited. After what seemed like a relatively short time, I felt myself Ascending the shaft of Light. I knew that I was still sitting in my meditation chair, but an aspect of my consciousness was moving through the shaft of Light into the dimensions of Light above me. I reached a place that clearly seemed to be what the mystery schools describe as the *Pure Land of Boundless Splendor and Infinite Light.*

In this dimension, my conscious mind effortlessly opened to greater levels of wisdom and a deeper understanding of reality. I began to remember amazing things that I realized I already knew, but that I had forgotten. No one was teaching me these things; I was just remembering. I sat for what seemed like hours absorbing everything that was surfacing into my conscious mind. Words cannot adequately describe the wonder and bliss I experienced during this glorious reconnection with my inner Truth.

After a time, I realized that Beloved Jesus was standing before me in his luminous Presence. He telepathically communicated to me that I was in the Realms of Illumined Truth, and that from this frequency of Divine Light I could communicate with any of the Beings of Light throughout the whole of Creation. He said that all I had to do was think of the Being I wanted to communicate with, and he or she would project their luminous Presence to me on the return current of consciousness.

I began by invoking Beloved Mother Mary. She is a Being of Light whom I have held in my heart for as far back as I can remember. Whenever I felt afraid or alone as a child, I sensed her tangible Presence and her loving embrace. Then I knew that I would be all right.

I followed Jesus' instructions, and the moment I thought of Mother Mary, she appeared before me. I realized that these Beings of Light have the ability to project their luminous Presence into the conscious minds of an infinite number of people simultaneously. They are powerful Suns of Light. When we ask them to intercede in our lives, they do not have to stop what they are doing to come and help us. They just project a ray of Light reflecting their luminous Presence into our energy field. They are then able to infuse us with whatever love, compassion, guidance, or assistance we need.

Jesus asked me to feel the frequency of vibration emanating from the luminous Presence of Mother Mary. He then asked me to call forth some of the other Beings of Light. I invoked the Beings I was familiar with who are associated with the other world religions: Krishna; Buddha; Moses; Mohammed; and Saint Germain, the Being of Light who is ushering in the Aquarian Age of Enlightenment and the Violet Flame of God's Infinite Perfection.

As the luminous Presence of these Beings appeared before me one by one, Jesus asked me to feel the frequency of their vibrations. It became very clear to me that each of these Beings has a very distinct vibration. Jesus said this is true for every Child of God, and that it is by our individual frequency of vibration that we are recognized in the Heavenly Realms.

Jesus revealed that every Child of God also has a musical keynote and a fragrance. He said that in the not-too-distant future, Humanity will develop our higher senses. Then we will recognize the vibration, keynote, and fragrance of all of our sisters and brothers in the Family of God

Jesus explained that this was a training session for me. He said it was important to develop the ability to recognize the Beings of Light in the Realms of Illumined Truth by their frequency of vibration. He said the purpose of this training was to empower me to be able to recognize the Beings of Light no matter where I was or what I was doing. The goal is for every Child of God to have a constant connection with the Realms of Illumined Truth, not only when we are in deep states of meditation but consistently throughout the day. That way, we will receive important guidance and insight into the things we are learning and experiencing as we go about the business of our daily lives.

The difficulty at this time is that when we are in this physical dimension, it is much easier for the mischievous souls who have temporarily chosen to remain in the psychic-astral plane, to project thoughtforms to us. Their thoughtforms are always intended to conflict with our Divine Plans, and they will lead us astray if we accept them as Truth.

These wayward souls have absolutely no power over the Light, and they cannot interfere in our lives unless we give them the ability to do so. They try to accomplish this by tricking us into believing that they are here to help us. They can say they are anybody. They can say they are Jesus, Mother Mary, Buddha, or any of the other Beings of Light. What they cannot do is emulate the frequency of vibration for these Beings. This is why it is important for each of us to learn to recognize the Beings of Light by their vibrations and not necessarily by whom they claim to be.

After a period of intense training and practice, I trusted my ability to identify the Beings of Light by their vibrations alone. Only then did I feel confident enough to begin looking for answers to the many questions I had about Humanity and our Earthly existence.

My questions were *Who are we? Where did we come from? Why are we here? How did we get into the mess we are in?* and *How will we get out of this mess?*

In the Realms of Illumined Truth, anything we could possibly want to know is available to us, but a very interesting thing happens when we are in that higher state of consciousness. A new level of integrity seems to awaken within us. We realize that the information we are receiving is a Sacred Trust between our God Selves, the Company of Heaven, and God.

With this knowing, we do not seek answers to frivolous questions just because we are curious. We do not invade other people's privacy by looking into their lives, even if we think the information might help them. We understand that it is interference for us to reveal things to people about their personal lives if their God Self has not already given them the information. We also do not try to predict the future or get numbers for the winning lottery ticket. With a higher level of integrity, we know that for us to do any of these things would be a sacrilege, an abuse of power, and a desecration of our sacred gift of Life.

Instead, we search for answers that will help us fulfill our purpose and reason for being on Earth in this lifetime. We know that we have had many lives, but in this higher consciousness they seem irrelevant. The only interest we have in our previous lives is to find out what we may have learned that will help us to accomplish our Divine Plan in this lifetime.

After contemplating these things for a while, I began my quest for answers in earnest. The things that were revealed to me during my many ventures into the Realms of Illumined Truth gave me a perspective about myself and this Earthly experience that transformed my way of thinking. In my estimation, this information is a priceless gift, and it is available to each and every one of us.

I am going to share this information with you now. The Divine Intent of my sharing is to awaken within you the remembrance of your own Divinity. My objective is to inspire you to seek the Kingdom of Heaven within your own heart, so that you will discover the answers to your questions. Then *you* will know who you are and why you are here.

# CHAPTER THREE

# THE BEGINNING

The Divine Intelligence we refer to as God is a radiant forcefield of pure Light that encompasses every particle and wave of Life in the whole of Creation. God is omnipotent, omniscient, and omnipresent. God is the Alpha—I—and the Omega—AM—the beginning and the ending—the Cosmic I AM. God is All That Is.

This Divine Intelligence pulsates with a masculine polarity and a feminine polarity. The masculine polarity is our Father God. This aspect of God radiates forth a sapphire blue frequency of Light that infuses all Creation with Divine Will, Power, and Authority. The feminine polarity is our Mother God. This aspect of God radiates forth a crystalline pink frequency of Light that infuses all Creation with Divine Love, Adoration, and Reverence for All Life. The activity of our Father God is the Outbreath of Creation. The activity of our Mother God is the Inbreath of Creation.

When the sapphire blue Light of our Father God and the crystalline pink Light of our Mother God are perfectly balanced, they merge into an unfathomable Sacred Fire. This Divine Flame is known through all Creation as the *Violet Flame of God's Infinite Perfection.*

Our Father-Mother God are whole and complete, but at some point in the evolutionary process they decided to create Sons and Daughters through which they could expand their love, adoration, and joy. The Children of God include you and me and every other Child of God throughout the whole of Creation. Our God Parents wanted us to learn to be cocreators with them, so they invested us with the gift of free will and the creative faculties of thought and feeling.

The Divine Plan was for the Children of God to observe all of the patterns of perfection existing in the Realms of Cause where everything begins, and then for us to create new expressions of Divinity by using our free will and our creative faculties of thought and feeling. Our Father-Mother God knew that by empowering their Children to become cocreators, we would expand the Body of God by creating previously unknown patterns of perfection and new learning experiences. Our God Parents realized that we would need vehicles in order to navigate through our schools of learning, so the process of creating our bodies began.

I never believed that I was just a physical body. I always knew that Human Beings are multifaceted and multidimensional, but I was shocked when I learned just how complex we are. At first, all of the details seemed confusing and maybe even unnecessary, but my inner guidance encouraged me to keep studying and not to give up. I kept going over the information, and little-by-little it began to make perfect sense.

Once I was familiar with all of the multidimensional facets of myself, I understood why the Beings of Light wanted me to have this knowledge. Just knowing about these various aspects of my Divinity opened the door for me to receive guidance and to communicate with a higher level of my consciousness. This helped immensely in my awakening process.

I am going to encourage you in the same way my inner guidance encouraged me. Please read the details about the various aspects of your Divinity and your Earthly bodies with an open heart and mind. If it seems too complicated, do not get frustrated. Just read it through and the seeds will be planted. At a later time, you can go over it again and you will be surprised how much easier it is for you to comprehend the importance of these various facets of yourself.

In the allegory of Adam and Eve, it is said that God created man—Adam—first. This symbolically demonstrates what occurs in the process of creation. The very first thing that happens when something is being created is that our Father God Outbreathes a Cosmic Tone, a Keynote, which forms the matrix for whatever is being created. *"In the beginning was the word, and the word was with God."*

It is said that woman—Eve—was created after Adam because once the matrix is formed by our Father God, our Mother God Inbreathes a ray of Divine Love into the *heart* of the matrix. Our Mother God's Love creates the cohesive power that magnetizes unformed primal Light into the matrix and holds it in the pattern for that particular creation. The symbology of the Adam and Eve story would have been more accurate if we had said that Eve came from Adam's heart instead of his rib.

In Divine Timing, our Father God began creating the matrixes for the vehicles of countless Sons and Daughters by sounding a Cosmic Tone. This Keynote reverberated through all Creation on the Outbreath of our Father God. Once this process was complete, our Mother God Inbreathed her Divine Love into the heart of each matrix. Her Love created the magnetic and the cohesive power to hold the primal Light for our various vehicles in their fixed patterns.

1. The first vehicle to form within our matrix was our *Immortal Victorious Threefold Flame.* This Sacred Fire consists of a Blue Flame, which represents the Power of our Father God; a Pink Flame, which represents Love of our Mother God; and a Yellow-gold Flame, which represents the Wisdom of the Son or Daughter of God—the Christ. Our *Immortal Vic-*

*torious Threefold Flame* is the *Holy Trinity*.

2. The next vehicle to form within our matrix was a blazing Sun, a radiant forcefield of pure Light that surrounded our Immortal Victorious Threefold Flame. This Sun with the Threefold Flame pulsating in its center is our *White Fire Being*. This is the aspect of our Divinity that is created in *"the Image and Likeness of God."*

3. The next vehicles to form within our matrix were our masculine and feminine *I AM Presences*. These are two radiant Beings of Light that represent the polarities of our Father God and our Mother God. Our masculine and feminine I AM Presences are *Divine Complements,* or *Twin Flames*.

Both of these aspects of our Divinity have an Immortal Victorious Threefold Flame, which forms their *Sacred Heart*. They also have a shaft of Divine Light that forms their spinal column; this is their *Solar Spine*. Pulsating along the Solar Spine are *Twelve Solar Chakras*. These Chakras are spheres of Light that radiate the *Twelve Solar Aspects of Deity* from the Causal Body of God.

The Twelve Solar Aspects of Deity pulsate with all of the patterns of perfection in the Causal Body of God. When they are unified into one powerful sphere of Light, as they are within the Twelve Solar Chakras of our I AM Presences, they are called the *Circle of the Sacred Twelve*. Here is a very brief description of the Twelve Solar Aspects of Deity in the Causal Body of God.

The **1st Solar Aspect of Deity** is sapphire blue and pulsates with the Divine Qualities of God's Will, Power, Illumined Faith, Protection, and God's First Cause of Perfection.

The **2nd Solar Aspect of Deity** is yellow-gold and pulsates with the Divine Qualities of Christ Consciousness, Enlightenment, Wisdom, Illumination, Understanding, and Perception.

The **3rd Solar Aspect of Deity** is crystalline pink and pulsates with the Divine Qualities of Transfiguring Divine Love, Acceptance, Adoration, and Reverence for ALL Life.

The **4th Solar Aspect of Deity** is white and pulsates with the Divine Qualities of Purity, Hope, the Immaculate Concept, Restoration, Resurrection, and Ascension.

The **5th Solar Aspect of Deity** is emerald green and pulsates with the Divine Qualities of Illumined Truth, Healing, Consecration, Concentration, and Inner Vision.

The **6th Solar Aspect of Deity** is ruby-gold and pulsates with the Divine Qualities of Ministering Grace, Healing, Devotional Worship, Peace, and The Christ Made Manifest.

The **7th Solar Aspect of Deity** is violet and pulsates with the Divine Qualities of Freedom, Liberty, Justice, Victory, Mercy, Compassion, Forgiveness, Transmutation, and God's Infinite Perfection.

The **8th Solar Aspect of Deity** is aquamarine and pulsates with the Divine Qualities of Clarity, Lucidity, Divine Perception, and Discernment.

The **9th Solar Aspect of Deity** is magenta and pulsates with the Divine Qualities of Harmony, Balance, Assurance, and Confidence.

The **10th Solar Aspect of Deity** is gold and pulsates with the Divine Qualities of Eternal Peace, Prosperity, Abundance, and the God Supply of ALL Good Things.

The **11th Solar Aspect of Deity** is peach and pulsates with the Divine Qualities of Purpose, Enthusiasm, and Joy.

The **12th Solar Aspect of Deity** is opal and pulsates with the Divine Qualities of Transformation and Transfiguration.

After our masculine and feminine I AM Presences with their Sacred Hearts, Solar Spines, and Twelve Solar Chakras were formed in our matrix, it was time for the creation of the next vehicles for the Children of God.

4. The next vehicles to form in our matrix were our *Causal Bodies*. These vehicles are large ovoids of Light that surround our I AM Presences. They are formed by the Light of the Twelve Solar Aspects of Deity flowing through the Chakras of our I AM Presences. Our *Causal Bodies* are multifaceted, multidimensional forcefields of Light that blaze in, through, and around our I AM Presences creating an aura of infinite Divine Potential. These are the vehicles through which we have access to every pattern of perfection in the Causal Body of God. This is why the Children of God are able to affirm the profound Truth, *"All that our Father-Mother God have is ours."*

In addition to all of the patterns of perfection in the Causal Body of God, every positive thought, word, feeling, or action we have expressed since our inception is stored in our Causal Body. This vehicle is referred to by the Company of Heaven as our *"storehouse of good."* Once we attain self-mastery and act out of our Divine Potential instead of the consciousness of our human ego, this storehouse of good will be released to us by our I AM Presence. Then we will cocreate Heaven on Earth, which is what our God Parents originally intended for us to cocreate.

# OUR DESCENT
# INTO THE WORLD OF FORM

After the creation of our *Immortal Victorious Threefold Flame*, *White Fire Being*, *I AM Presences*, and *Causal Bodies*, it was time for the next step in the evolutionary process of the Sons and Daughters of God.

Our Father-Mother God initially created their Children within the highest dimensions of Light. In these frequencies, there is no such thing as time or space. Only the Eternal Moment of Now is relevant. But our Father-Mother God wanted their Children to learn how to become cocreators as quickly as possible. In order for that to happen, we needed to experience what we were cocreating through our thoughts, words, feelings, and actions in an accelerated manner. It was determined that this would occur most effectively within the denser frequencies of a time and space continuum. This meant that we needed to step our vehicles down into denser frequencies of vibration.

To begin this process, our Father-Mother God decreed that the aspect of our Divinity that was created in the image and likeness of God would remain within the highest dimensions of God's Infinite Light. This was our White Fire Being and the Immortal Victorious Threefold Flame blazing in its center. This step was taken in order to ensure our safe return when our learning experiences were complete. Our God Parents invested our White Fire Beings with the responsibility of holding the Immaculate Concept—the Divine Blueprint—for our descent into the 3rd-Dimensional world of form, and our ascent back into the Heart of our Father-Mother God.

Next our God Parents directed our masculine and feminine I AM Presences to descend into the densest dimension they could abide in while still remaining in the timeless, spaceless frequencies of Light. This was the 5th Dimension.

After our I AM Presences were established in the frequencies of the 5th Dimension, our Father-Mother God directed them to project a stepped-down reflection of themselves into the denser frequencies of the 4th Dimension. The 4th Dimension is the first dimension that exists within a time and space continuum. It is much more rarified than the 3rd Dimension, but it exists within the initial constraints of time and space.

In compliance with the request of our Father-Mother God, our I AM Presences projected stepped-down masculine and feminine reflections of themselves into the 4th Dimension. These two aspects of our Divinity are called our *Solar Christ Presences*.

Like our I AM Presences, our Solar Christ Presences have a Sacred Heart with a Threefold Flame, a Solar Spine, and Twelve Solar Chakras. Because the 4th Dimension is so much denser than the 5th Dimension, the Twelve Solar Aspects of Deity reflect differently through the twelve Chakras of our Solar Christ Presences. Instead of all Twelve Aspects of Deity radiating out through each of the twelve Chakras as they do in our I AM Presences, in our Solar Christ Presences only one of the Twelve Aspects of Deity radiates through each Chakra. Since each Chakra reflects only one Aspect of Deity, all twelve Chakras must function together in order to form the Circle of the Sacred Twelve.

After our Solar Christ Presences were securely established in the 4th Dimension, the Sons and Daughters of God were ready for the final step of our descent into matter. This would involve our descent into the 3rd Dimension, which would be the most critical and the most difficult part of our journey.

Our Father-Mother God directed our masculine and feminine Solar Christ Presences to project stepped-down reflections of themselves into the 3rd Dimension. This was the densest and the most compressed frequency of time and space that the Children of God would have to experience in order to become cocreators. These two aspects of our Divinity are called our *Planetary Christ Presences*.

A dramatic change occurs when Light passes from the prism of the 4th Dimension into the 3rd Dimension. When the 4th-Dimensional frequency of Solar Light is compressed into an even denser 3rd-Dimensional frequency, the Solar Light is transformed into the pigment octave of physical Light. We witness this when we pass a ray of Sunlight through the prism of a crystal. The Solar Light is condensed into the sevenfold spectrum of physical Light, and we see a rainbow on the other side of the crystal.

When our Solar Christ Presences projected reflections of themselves into the 3rd Dimension to create our Planetary Christ Presences, the same thing happened. Instead of our Planetary Christ Presences having twelve Chakras in the frequencies of the 3rd Dimension, they have only seven Chakras. These Chakras reflect the seven colors of the rainbow beginning with the red Root Chakra at the base of the spine and ending with the violet Crown Chakra at the top of the head.

In the physical plane, our male and female Planetary Christ Presences evolve as two separate Human Beings. These 3rd-Dimensional aspects of ourselves are also called Divine Complements, or Twin Flames. They belong to the same White Fire Being, but they evolve through separate Earthly experiences. If you are learning about this for the first time, it may seem shocking that there is another aspect of yourself evolving on this planet, but do not let this overwhelm you. This has always been the case, and you are well aware of this Truth within your higher consciousness.

There is one cautionary note I would like to mention about Twin Flames. People are awakening and beginning to remember that they have a Twin Flame somewhere. This is causing them to ask questions about how they should interact with this other aspect of themselves. Unfortunately, the available information is often confusing. There are people who are teaching that we must seek out our Twin Flame in order to develop a romantic relationship with this counterpart of ourselves. People are being taught that if we are not in a romantic relationship with our Twin Flame, it is like trying to fly with one wing, and that we will not be able to reach our highest potential. This belief is inaccurate and actually distracts us from fulfilling our Divine Plans. I would like to take a moment to share with you what the Beings of Light have revealed to Humanity about Twin Flames.

The Company of Heaven has said that it is inappropriate for us to spend our energy searching for our Twin Flame in order to have a romantic relationship with him or her in this lifetime. Traditionally, Twin Flames choose not to embody at the same time. This way, one can assist from On High while the other is going through his or her Earthly lessons.

If Twin Flames do embody at the same time, they often choose lifepaths that would prevent them from having a romantic relationship. Even though one Planetary Christ Presence reflects the masculine polarity of God and the other reflects the feminine polarity of God, this does not mean that the masculine Christ Presence is always a man or that the feminine Christ Presence is always a woman. On the contrary, they both go through the full gamut of experiences on Earth in order to learn to be cocreators.

In this evolutionary process, our Christ Presences have chosen to be both men and women myriad times. They have also chosen to experience every race, religion, nationality, culture, creed, and lifestyle available on this planet. If they do happen to know each other in a particular lifetime, they may be the wrong chronological age or the wrong gender or related in ways they would prevent them from being romantically involved. Your Twin Flame might be your mother or your child or someone on the other side of the planet whom you will never even meet in this lifetime.

Very rarely, we are blessed with the opportunity to be with our Twin Flame in a loving, romantic relationship for a specific learning experience in a particular lifetime. Know that if such a relationship is destined to be, it will occur naturally and unexpectedly without any deliberate searching on your part. Such a relationship is a gift that should be deeply cherished and revered.

Regardless of what the circumstance of our Twin Flame is, we are always united with this aspect of our Divinity through our White Fire Being. We have the ability to ask our Twin Flame for assistance, and we can communicate with him or her through open-heart-and-mind telepathic communication any time we choose to do so.

When all of our lessons are complete, we will Ascend back into our White Fire Being. Within this radiant Sun, we will be reunited with our Twin Flame for all Eternity. In the meantime, we must stay on purpose and fulfill whatever it is we volunteered to accomplish in this lifetime.

# THE CREATION OF OUR
# SOLAR SYSTEM

The intent of this book is to remind us of who we are and why we are on Earth at this time. To fully understand this, we need to know how the Earth got into her present predicament. There are many scenarios that have been reported throughout the Ages, but most of them are based in fear and expound on our human frailties. The information being given to Humanity at this time by the Beings of Light in the Realms of Illumined Truth is different. These Beings have come through the veil to meet us halfway, and Humanity is reaching up in consciousness and learning a new perspective from our highly evolved sisters and brothers. The Truth we are grasping now is wondrous and amazing. We are beginning to perceive the bigger picture with a new level of clarity and understanding.

Let's begin with a very condensed version of the creation of our Solar System. There are billions of Universes throughout the whole of Creation, within which the Sons and Daughters of God are learning to become cocreators. Each Universe is unique, and they are all experiencing different degrees of development. Due to the need of the hour, I am going to focus on the Solar System in which the Earth is evolving. This will help us to comprehend the magnitude of what is happening on this planet during the unprecedented experiment we are all going through.

The Beings of Light have given us details about the Suns and planets in our Solar System. This information seems to conflict with what our scientists are able to perceive with their 3rd-Dimensional instruments. The reason for this will be explained as I share with you what is being revealed from On High.

The creation of every Solar System begins with a Central Sun. This spiritual Sun, which is sometimes referred to as *"the Sun behind the Sun,"* is actually the White Fire Being of a Son and Daughter of God who have completed their lessons of cocreation and decided that they would like to be responsible for cocreating a Solar System. That may seem astounding, but it is one of the myriad opportunities that are available to the Children of God in our evolutionary process. The White Fire Being that forms our Central Sun belongs to the Beings known as Alpha and Omega. Alpha and Omega are the *Solar Logos* of our Central Sun.

When Alpha and Omega decided that they would like to cocreate a Solar System, they asked permission from our Father-Mother God. Once permission was granted, they determined what patterns of perfection from the Causal Body of God they wanted to have as the predominant focus of learning for the Sons and Daughters of God who would be evolving in their system of worlds.

Alpha and Omega chose to focus on the *Twelve Solar Aspects of Deity*. They decided that this Solar System would consist of twelve physical Suns and that each Sun would reflect all of the Twelve Solar Aspects of Deity. This meant that all twelve Suns would sustain the *Circle of the Sacred Twelve* for the planets that would evolve under their radiance.

The next thing Alpha and Omega decided was that each of the twelve Suns would be responsible for twelve 3rd-Dimensional planets upon which the Children of God would evolve. With this decision, the sacred geometry for the Solar System of Alpha and Omega was set in place. This system would express the power of the 12 X 12—144; twelve Suns radiating Twelve Solar Aspects of Deity—144; and twelve planets evolving around each of the twelve Suns—144.

Once these decisions were made, Alpha and Omega sent forth a clarion call asking for volunteers who were interested in having their White Fire Being serve as one of the twelve physical Suns in this system. From the many volunteers, Alpha and Omega chose twelve Sons and Daughters of God who had completed their lessons of cocreation and were once again living within their White Fire Being. These selfless Beings of Light agreed to be responsible for the evolution of twelve planets. They made the commitment to hold each of the twelve planets in the radiance of the Twelve Solar Aspects of Deity until the Children of God evolving on these planets completed their lessons of cocreation.

When the time was right, Alpha and Omega breathed the White Fire Beings of those who had volunteered to be the twelve Suns in our system into their strategic positions in the Universe. The physical Sun to which the Earth belongs is the White Fire Being of Helios and Vesta. Helios and Vesta are the *Solar Logos* of our physical Sun, which is the fourth Sun out from the Central Sun of Alpha and Omega.

The next step in the process was for the Solar Logos of the twelve Suns to ask for volunteers who were interested in having their White Fire Being serve as a planet in this Solar System. One hundred forty-four Sons and Daughters of God were chosen who had completed their lessons of cocreation and were living within their White Fire Beings.

When the time was right, Helios and Vesta and the eleven other physical Suns, breathed into place the White Fire Beings of the 144 planets. These selfless volunteers form the *Sun of Even Pressure,* which pulsates as the magnetic crystalline core within each planet. The Beings whose White Fire Being forms the Sun of Even Pressure in the center of the Earth are Pelleur and Virgo. The Earth is the fourth planet out from the Sun of Helios and Vesta.

After the Sun of Even Pressure was in place for each planet, Alpha and Omega summoned the Builders of Form, the mighty Elohim. These majestic Beings are responsible for the Elemental Kingdom. The Elementals are the intelligent Lifeforms who cocreate the earth, air, water, fire, and ether elements from unformed primal Light.

In compliance with the decree of Alpha and Omega, the Elohim directed the Elementals to create a verdant paradise of splendor on all 144 planets. On Earth this pristine beauty was known as the *Garden of Eden*. In the beginning, everything the Children of God needed to sustain our Earthly bodies and to learn our lessons of cocreation was supplied by the Elemental Kingdom in great abundance.

When all was in readiness, Alpha and Omega called forth the 3rd-Dimensional Christ Selves of the Sons and Daughters of God who wanted to learn to become cocreators through the lessons of the Twelve Solar Aspects of Deity. Billions and billions of Christ Selves responded to the call and entered the White Fire Being of Alpha and Omega.

To begin the process of embodiment, the Christ Selves were divided into seven Root Races, and each Root Race was divided into seven Subraces. At the appropriate time, Alpha and Omega sounded a Cosmic Tone signaling to the Solar System that it was time for the Christ Selves from the First Subrace of the First Root Race to embody on all 144 planets. The White Fire Being of each of the twelve physical Suns stood in readiness to receive the first Christ Selves who would embody on their twelve planets.

On the Holy Breath, Alpha and Omega breathed the First

Subrace of the First Root Race into the White Fire Being of the specific Sun that would be responsible for their evolution. In Divine Timing, the very first Christ Selves to embody in the Solar System of Alpha and Omega were escorted into the physical plane on all 144 planets.

The Christ Selves were accompanied by numerous teachers and guides from the Realms of Illumined Truth. They were also gifted with the assistance of legions of Angels and Elemental Beings. These selfless Beings of Light agreed to remain with the Christ Selves until they completed their Earthly lessons of becoming cocreators.

## OUR CHRIST SELF'S
## EARTHLY BODIES

Our 3rd-Dimensional Planetary Christ Presence is the aspect of our Divinity that abides in the physical plane. For our purposes here I am going to call this aspect of ourselves our *"Christ Self."*

In the beginning, our Christ Self was a full-grown Being of Light, and our Immortal Victorious Threefold Flame enveloped our Christ Self's Light Body. The Blue Flame of our Father God's Power activated our left-brain hemisphere and the rational, logical portion of our brain. It also activated the power center within our Throat Chakra. The Pink Flame of our Mother God's Love activated our right-brain hemisphere and the creative, intuitive portion of our brain. This Sacred Fire also activated the love center within our Heart Chakra.

Within our Christ Self, the masculine and the feminine polarities of our Father-Mother God were perfectly balanced. This allowed our Father God's Blue Flame of Power and our Mother God's Pink Flame of Love to merge into the *Violet Flame of*

*God's Infinite Perfection.*

This perfectly balanced frequency of Light activated our spiritual brain centers, which are our pituitary, pineal, hypothalamus glands, and the ganglionic centers at the base of our brain. When these spiritual brain centers were activated, our Crown Chakra opened allowing the Yellow-gold Flame of Christ Consciousness to expand within our Christ Self. This completed our Immortal Victorious Threefold Flame and the manifestation of the *Holy Trinity* within us.

In the beginning, our Christ Self lived, moved, and breathed within a shaft of Light. This pillar of Light extended from the Heart of God into the center of the Earth. It kept our Christ Self directly connected to all of our aspects of Divinity: our Solar Christ Presence, I AM Presence, Causal Body, White Fire Being, and the entire Company of Heaven. This shaft of Light radiated through the spinal column of our Christ Self activating our Sevenfold Chakra System. The sevenfold spectrum of physical Light that flowed through our planetary Chakras formed a scintillating aura of color all around us.

Our Christ Self was invested with a gift from our Father-Mother God that would enable us to function in the 3rd Dimension while remaining fully connected to all of the aspects of Divinity in the Realms of Perfection. We were given twelve Solar Strands of DNA. This complex DNA was designed to function as a very elaborate communication system. The intent was to keep our Christ Self connected to the Twelve Solar Aspects of Deity even though we were limited to a Sevenfold Chakra System.

After receiving our twelve Solar Strands of DNA, our Christ Self was ready to create the four Earthly bodies we would need in order to learn the lessons of cocreation in the 3rd Dimension. This would require the full cooperation of the Elemental Kingdom. The first step in this process was for the Elohim to elect an Elemental Being who would agree to remain with our Christ Self through all of our Earthly sojourns. The mission of this selfless servant of our Father-Mother God was to provide our Christ Self with Earthly bodies that would maintain vibrant health and eternal youth. The plan was for our Christ Self to learn the lessons of cocreation without being distracted with the struggle of keeping our physical bodies healthy and alive. This Being is our *Body Elemental.* Once the Body Elemental was assigned to our Christ Self, it established the five Elemental Vortices that would energize and rejuvenate our Earthly bodies on a daily basis.

1. The first to be established was the *Ether Vortex.* This vortex pulsates above our head and bathes our Christ Self in a forcefield of rarified ethers that pulsate with the Divine Potential of limitless physical perfection.

2. The next vortex to be established was the *Air Vortex.* This vortex pulsates in the area of our Christ Self's Throat Chakra. The unformed primal Light for the *etheric body* of our Christ Self is magnetized and held into place through this vortex. Our etheric body is associated with the air element.

Our etheric body interpenetrates every cell and organ and extends a little beyond our physical body. It is comprised of very sensitive chemical ethers that record every thought, word, feeling, and action expressed by our Christ Self. This vehicle is considered *"the seat of all memory."* The portion of our etheric body that contains all of our etheric records and memories remains with our Christ Self lifetime after lifetime.

3. The next vortex to be established was the *Fire Vortex.* This vortex pulsates in the area of our Christ Self's Heart Chakra. The unformed primal Light for the *mental body* of

our Christ Self is magnetized and held into place through this vortex. Our mental body is associated with the fire element.

The intent of our mental body is to keep our Christ Self connected with the Divine Mind of God and the Realms of Thought. This vehicle allows us to effectively utilize our creative faculties of thought while we are learning to become cocreators.

There is a lot of discussion at this time as to whether the brain and the mind are the same thing, or if they are two separate entities. The Beings of Light have revealed that our mind, which is our mental body, and our physical brain are two separate entities. Our mental body functions in alignment with the Divine Mind of God and the Realms of Thought. This vehicle is always whole and complete.

Our physical brain is the instrument through which our mental body expresses thoughts in the physical plane. Our physical brain can be damaged or chemically unbalanced, which causes mental illness and prevents us from clearly expressing thoughts, but this does not affect our mental body. Even if a person is in a coma or unable to express thoughts in any way, the mental body is still processing the experience of that person and everything is being recorded in the etheric body. Nothing in our Earthly experience is ever lost, regardless of outer appearances.

4. The next vortex to be established by our Body Elemental was the *Water Vortex*. This vortex pulsates in the area of our Christ Self's Root Chakra, at the base of the spine. The unformed primal Light for the *emotional body* of our Christ Self is magnetized and held into place through this vortex. Our emotional body is associated with the water element.

This is our largest Earthly vehicle. Our emotional body surrounds our physical body and extends for several feet in every direction. Approximately eighty percent of the energy we release is expressed through our emotional body. The remaining twenty percent is expressed through our thoughts, words, and actions.

5.   The fifth and final vortex to be established by our Body Elemental was the *Earth Vortex*. This vortex pulsates in the area between the feet of our Christ Self. The unformed primal Light for the *physical body* of our Christ Self is magnetized and held into place through this vortex. This vortex grounds our Christ Self in the physical plane and allows us to easily navigate around in the 3rd Dimension. Our physical body is associated with the earth element.

Our physical body, is merely the car that we drive while abiding on Earth; it is not who we are. Over aeons of time and through myriad lifetimes our Christ Self has chosen physical bodies that would allow us to experience both genders, as well as every race, religion, nationality, culture, creed, and lifestyle existing on Earth. We have also experienced every possible situation and condition on this planet.

The original Divine Plan was for our Body Elemental to observe the perfection of our Christ Self's Light Body, and then to create Earthly bodies that reflected that perfection. Once our Earthly bodies were created, it was the responsibility of the Body Elemental to maintain and sustain our bodies in states of vibrant health and eternal youth. Our Body Elemental accomplished this by magnetizing primal Light into our Earthly bodies every day through our Elemental Vortices.

The Divine Intent was for our Christ Self to be able to learn the lessons of cocreation without being distracted with the challenges of aging and disease.

With the establishment of our five Elemental Vortices and the creation of our etheric, mental, emotional, and physical bodies, our Christ Self was ready to begin the lessons of cocreation.

# CHAPTER FOUR

# LEARNING TO BE
# A COCREATOR

Once the Christ Selves of the First Subrace of the First Root Race were embodied on all 144 planets in the Solar System of Alpha and Omega, and their Body Elementals had created their Elemental Vortices and their Earthly bodies, it was time for the learning experiences of cocreation to begin.

At that time, the Sons and Daughters of God were consciously aware of the covenant we had made with our Father-Mother God. In that covenant, our God Parents agreed to provide us with our Lifeforce and everything we needed to effortlessly sustain our Earthly bodies in the 3rd Dimension. The infinite abundance of God was our Divine Birthright, and our lessons of cocreation were a joy-filled experience in a verdant paradise of splendor. We remained consciously connected to the various aspects of our own Divinity, and we had access to the patterns of perfection in the Causal Body of God. Our Father-Mother God's part of the covenant also included the guidance of the entire Company of Heaven, including the Angelic and Elemental Kingdoms.

In return, the Children of God agreed to fulfill our part of the covenant. We understood that there is a balance that must be maintained between the Outbreath and the Inbreath of Creation. The gifts our God Parents agreed to provide for us in their part of the covenant involved the Outbreath of Creation. The agreements we made to fulfill our part of the covenant involved the Inbreath of Creation.

We agreed that we would use our free will and our creative faculties of thought and feeling to cocreate patterns of perfection from the Causal Body of God in the physical plane of Earth. We agreed that we would experiment with cocreating new patterns of perfection that would expand the borders of the Kingdom of Heaven on Earth. We agreed to revere every facet of Life and to love and respect the Elemental Kingdom for their selfless service to Humanity. We agreed to cocreate with the clear understanding of our Oneness with all Life. We promised to honor the Divinity within the hearts of the other Christ Selves we would be learning and growing with on this planet. We pledged to remember that every atomic and subatomic particle and wave of our Lifeforce is intelligent Life that we must never desecrate or misuse in any way.

To insure that the lessons of cocreation for the Christ Selves evolving in the system of Alpha and Omega would always be joyful and glorious, our Father-Mother God gave one commandment:

*"Do not partake of the tree of knowledge*
*of good and evil."*

Our Father-Mother God knew that if we had no knowledge of the human miscreations that had been created long ago by our sisters and brothers in other systems of worlds, we would not recreate these painful experiences in the Solar System of Alpha and Omega. If we had no knowledge of poverty, greed, corruption, violence, war, hunger, disease, or any other humanly created form of pain and suffering, these things would simply not be part of our consciousness. Therefore, we would not cocreate them with our thoughts and feelings.

There was a reason why our Father-Mother God felt the need to warn us to avoid partaking of the tree of knowledge of good and evil. We have all heard the allegory of Lucifer and the fallen Angels, but much of this story has been misunderstood. It is true that in other Solar Systems, long before Alpha and Omega cocreated this system, some of the Children of God chose to use their free will and their creative faculties of thought and feeling in ways that conflicted with the patterns of perfection in the Causal Body of God. Instead of expanding the Body of God, these Sons and Daughters created gross mutations that resulted in all manner of pain and suffering.

It is said that in God's wrath, Lucifer and the fallen Angels were cast out of Heaven, but that is not how God responds. Our Father-Mother God never judge or punish us, and they are certainly never wrathful. These Supreme Beings do not release one electron of precious Life energy that is less than pure Divine Love. They do, however, allow us to experience the results of our free-will choices and our thoughts and feelings.

The distorted mutations created by these Children of God caused very destructive frequencies of vibration, which interpenetrated their etheric, mental, emotional, and physical bodies. The negative vibrations caused these souls to fall below the frequencies of harmony and balance in the Causal Body of God. Our Father-Mother God would not project one electron of precious Life energy into these discordant frequencies to sustain these souls. The only way they could survive was to find another source of energy that they could live off of parasitically.

These fallen souls roamed the Universe looking for innocent Sons and Daughters of God that they could entice into creating negative thoughts, words, feelings, and actions. They would then absorb these discordant frequencies of vibration to keep themselves alive.

This scenario is what is symbolically depicted in the allegory of Adam and Eve. In that depiction, we see the serpent entwined in the tree of knowledge of good and evil as it tries to entice Eve into eating the apple.

For a while, everything went as planned in the system of Alpha and Omega. The Christ Selves evolving on Earth used our free will and our thoughts and feelings as our Father-Mother God originally intended. Each day we would observe the patterns of perfection in the Causal Body of God and say to ourselves, *"How shall I use my gift of Life today to expand the Kingdom of Heaven on Earth? How shall I cocreate new patterns of perfection to expand the Body of God?"*

We gratefully received our Lifeforce as it flowed from the Heart of God through our shaft of Light. This precious gift of Life entered our Crown Chakra and descended into our Immortal Victorious Threefold Flame. Within our Heart Flame this electronic Light substance was imprinted with our Christ Self's *individual electronic pattern.* This electronic Light pattern is unique for every Child of God. This is how the Universe determines what energy belongs to whom. Once our Lifeforce was imprinted with our individual pattern, the atomic and subatomic particles and waves of energy contained within this gift of Life were available for us to use as we went about the business of our daily lives.

With every thought, feeling, word, or action our Christ Self expressed, our Lifeforce was sent forth on an electromagnetic current of energy. This current of energy contained whatever frequency of vibration our Christ Self charged it with depending on our thoughts and feelings at the time.

In the beginning our thoughts and feelings were always positive. They were filled with love, harmony, peace, and balance. We had no awareness of the human miscreations that our sisters and brothers in other Solar Systems had created, so the focus of our attention was held exclusively on the patterns of perfection in the Causal Body of God.

As the current of energy from our thoughts and feelings passed through the atmosphere, it magnetized to itself other energy that was vibrating at the same frequency. In the laws of physics, like attracts like. This had the effect of making our current of energy much more powerful. For instance, when we sent forth a feeling of love, it passed through the atmosphere accumulating other frequencies of love along the way. By the time our current of love reached its destination, it was greatly amplified over what we had originally sent out. This amplified frequency of love blessed everything in its path as it flowed into the experience of the person, place, condition, or thing to which it was sent.

This phase of our Lifeforce's journey is called *involution*. Involution begins in the Heart of God, and culminates when our Lifeforce reaches the furthest point of its destination in the physical world of form. After our Lifeforce completes the path of involution, it must return to the Source. This phase of the journey is called *evolution,* and it completes the Law of the Circle.

In the beginning, the Law of the Circle was an experience of joy. During the *evolutionary* phase of the journey, our Lifeforce was magnetized back to the electronic Light pattern in our Heart Flame. This pattern was the identical electronic Light pattern that had been imprinted on the energy of our Lifeforce when we first received it from the Heart of God.

On the return journey back to our Heart Flame, our current of love, once again, accumulated energy that was vibrating at the same frequency. When this greatly amplified current of love reentered our Heart Flame, it blessed our Christ Self and everything in its path with love.

Our current of love then passed through our Heart Flame on its return journey back to the Heart of God. On the way, our Lifeforce passed through our Causal Body, where all of the patterns of love it had accumulated were recorded in our storehouse of good. The covenant between our Father-Mother God and our Christ Self was fulfilled through this involutionary and evolutionary process of our Lifeforce—the Law of the Circle.

In the original Divine Plan, the Christ Selves of the First Subrace of the First Root Race in the system of Alpha and Omega went through all of the lifetimes and experiences necessary in order to learn the 3rd-Dimensional lessons of cocreation. Each lifetime lasted between 800 and 900 years. During that time, the Christ Selves experienced the results of their thoughts, feelings, words, and actions. They clearly perceived the patterns of perfection they were learning to cocreate.

The Christ Selves alternated between male and female physical bodies in various lifetimes. This allowed them to experience different things, and to cocreate different patterns of perfection. All of the lessons learned in one lifetime were consciously remembered in the next lifetime, so progress was on-going.

After many lifetimes and thousands of years, the Christ Selves of the First Subrace of the First Root Race completed their lessons of cocreation in the 3rd Dimension. With this victorious accomplishment, the Christ Selves Ascended the spiral of evolution into the 4th Dimension, and became One with their Solar Christ Presences. In this more rarified frequency of Light, they commenced the next phase of their evolutionary process back to the Heart of God.

After the Ascension of the First Subrace, the Christ Selves of the Second Subrace of the First Root Race embodied in the 3rd Dimension to begin their lessons of cocreation. For millions of years this process unfolded Subrace by Subrace in perfect Divine Order. Then something happened that changed the course of history for Planet Earth and the entire Solar System of Alpha and Omega. In the middle of the evolutionary process for the Fourth Subrace of the Fourth Root Race, the Universe experienced what is known as *the Shift of the Ages*.

## THE SHIFT OF THE AGES

The Shift of the Ages is a rare moment in time that occurs only once in many millions of years. This event involves a unique alignment during which celestial and galactic cycles within cycles within cycles throughout the whole of Creation dovetail into one synchronized pulsation. This event rhythmically unifies all Life everywhere for one Cosmic Moment.

During this awesome moment, every particle of Life existing in the Body of God pulsates in unison with the Cosmic Heartbeat of our omniscient, omnipresent, omnipotent Father-Mother God—All That Is. In that instant, our Father-Mother God Inbreathe all Life up the Spiral of Evolution into the next octave of Divine Potential. This Inbreath creates a shift of energy, vibration, and consciousness that catapults all Creation a quantum leap forward in the Light.

Here are just a few of the grand cycles involved in the Shift of the Ages: the 26,000-year Precession of the Equinoxes; the 438,000-year cycle called Kali Yuga; the 1.8 million-year cycle called Satya Yuga; the 4.4 million-year cycle called Mahayuga; and the 4.4 billion-year cycle called Kalpa, or the Day of Brahma. A Kalpa equals 1,000 Mahayugas or Divine Ages, a major Universal cycle. The Day of Brahma reverberates with the prime creative force of the Godhead. This cycle is one day in the *"seven days of Creation"* mentioned in the Bible.

In the middle of the evolutionary process for the Christ Selves in the system of Alpha and Omega, the alignment for the Shift of the Ages occurred. At that time, the Earth was evolving as the pristine Garden of Eden. No one on this planet had partaken of the tree of knowledge of good and evil. This meant that the Earth and all Life evolving upon her could be easily Inbreathed up the Spiral of Evolution into the next octave of our Divine Potential. Since we were evolving in the 3rd Dimension, this Inbreath for the Shift of the Ages would lift the Solar System of Alpha and Omega into the 4th Dimension.

Not all of the planets in the system of Alpha and Omega were in the same situation as the Earth. Unfortunately, some of the Children of God evolving on some of the remaining 143 planets had been enticed into partaking of the tree of knowledge of good and evil. These souls had experienced a tragic fall from Grace, and they were vibrating at discordant frequencies that would not be able to withstand the higher vibrations of the 4th Dimension.

Everything existing in the whole of Creation is comprised of energy, vibration, and consciousness. The Inbreath associated with the Shift of the Ages breathes all Life into much higher frequencies of vibration. If for some reason, a Child of God is vibrating at a discordant frequency that cannot survive the Inbreath involved in the Shift of the Ages, that Son or Daughter of God is left behind. This is not punishment by our Father-Mother God. It happens because the person would not survive the transition into the higher frequencies of Light. It would be like him or her trying to pass through a lightning bolt.

Being left behind during the Shift of the Ages is considered the most tragic thing that can happen to a Son or Daughter of God. It means that person loses the opportunity to advance with the rest of the Christ Selves in their Solar System. Nothing is ever totally lost, but when a soul is left behind, his or her evolution is delayed for aeons of time.

The souls who are left behind are returned to their Central Sun, where they are held in a state of limbo until the opportunity is presented for them to embody in another Solar System. That system must be vibrating at a frequency that is dense enough to receive the misqualified energy and the karmic liabilities these souls created. They are obligated to take all of their human miscreations with them into embodiment. The purpose of this is to allow the souls to experience the results of their previous thoughts, feelings, words, and actions, and to provide them with the opportunity to transmute these miscreations back into Light.

Usually these souls are reborn at the caveman level of consciousness. This, tragically, sets their evolution back millions of years. This step is taken in order to prevent them from immediately destroying themselves with destructive technology. Even though these fallen souls have a caveman's level of consciousness, there is no guarantee that they will work with the Light. They still have the free will to create all manner of pain and suffering for themselves and the souls abiding with them on the new planet.

When the Children of God evolving on Earth became aware that many of their sisters and brothers from some of the other planets in this Solar System were going to be left behind during the Shift of the Ages, they wanted to do something to help them. After much deliberation the Christ Selves on Earth came up with a plan. They appealed to Alpha and Omega and asked for permission to implement an experiment that had never been attempted. This experiment involved the greatest compassion, love, and sacrifice that any of the Sons and Daughters of God had ever expressed for their sisters and brothers.

# THE  EXPERIMENT

At the time of the Shift of the Ages, the Earth was fulfilling the Immaculate Concept of the original Divine Plan for the Solar System of Alpha and Omega. No one on this planet had partaken of the tree of knowledge of good and evil, so none of the humanly created patterns of pain and suffering existed here. Contrary to what we have come to believe, it was *never* our Father-Mother God's intent that we use our free will to choose between cocreating good or evil. The original Divine Plan for this Solar System was specifically designed to help us avoid experiencing the gross mutations of disease, aging, poverty, war, hatred, hunger, violence, corruption, greed, and every other human miscreation that our fallen sisters and brothers in other systems of worlds had created through their abuse of power and the misuse of their creative faculties of thought and feeling.

On Earth, our free will was being used as our God Parents intended. We were choosing each day how we would use our Lifeforce to cocreate new patterns of perfection. The patterns we were cocreating involved previously unknown expressions of love, beauty, music, art, dance, wisdom, happiness, joy, enlightenment, and myriad other glorious things from the plethora of Divine patterns existing in the Causal Body of God. We were well aware of the Oneness of all Life. We knew how to effectively use our creative faculties of thought and feeling in ways that would add to the Light of the world and in ways that would always result in the highest good for all Life.

Since the Christ Selves on Earth had never experienced negativity, we had no concept of what human miscreations our sisters and brothers on the other planets had manifested. All we knew was that these Children of God were about to be left behind, and we wanted to do whatever we could to prevent that tragic event. We believed that if we had the opportunity to love these fallen souls enough, we would be able to lift them up and guide them back to the path of Light. So in an act of unprecedented Divine Love, the people evolving on Earth presented our plan to Alpha and Omega.

We asked Alpha and Omega if they would allow all of the souls in this Solar System who were going to be left behind during the Shift of the Ages to be transferred to the Earth. Our plan was for the Earth to temporarily remain in the 3rd Dimension, where we could hold the sacred space for these souls until they remembered their Divine Birthright as Beloved Sons and Daughters of God. Our goal was to love them and guide them back to the path of Oneness and Reverence for All Life. We believed that if we could do this effectively, the fallen souls would change their course of direction. Then we would all be able to Ascend into the 4th Dimension and catch up with the rest of our Solar System. This plan meant that instead of being left behind, the fallen souls with all of their misqualified energy and all of their karmic liabilities would embody on planet Earth.

Alpha and Omega knew that the Children of Earth had no idea what we were getting ourselves into, but our whole purpose and reason for being was to cocreate new patterns of perfection. Since that magnitude of Divine Love had never been demonstrated by the Sons and Daughters of God in any system of worlds, no one knew if we would be able to succeed in cocreating this selfless plan of Divine Love. With the greatest of expectations, Alpha and Omega agreed to allow us to attempt this mighty feat.

To help with this holy endeavor, Alpha and Omega issued a Cosmic Dispensation giving the Company of Heaven permission to assist us the maximum that Cosmic Law would allow. This had to be done, of course, without interfering with our free will. Helios and Vesta agreed to help by sustaining the Earth in the 3rd Dimension while the experiment was implemented. Members of the Angelic and Elemental Kingdoms agreed to stay behind with us, in order to assist in any way they could with this unprecedented experiment of Divine Love.

When the moment arrived for the Shift of the Ages, our omniscient, omnipotent, omnipresent Father-Mother God—All That Is—sounded a Cosmic Tone. This tone signaled that all Creation was aligned with the rhythmic heartbeat of the Cosmic I AM. Our Father-Mother God then Inbreathed all Life up the Spiral of Evolution into the next octave of Divine Potential. The twelve Suns and 143 of the planets in the Solar System of Alpha and Omega were breathed into the 4th Dimension. The Earth alone remained in the 3rd Dimension.

During the Cosmic Inbreath, the fallen souls who were destined to be left behind were transferred to the inner planes of Earth. There they entered the schools of learning that would prepare them for their eventual embodiment on this planet.

The 4th Dimension vibrates at a frequency that transcends our 3rd-Dimensional physical sight. This is why our Solar System appears to be different from what the Beings of Light have revealed to us. The planets we see with our physical sight are the planets that are in the closest proximity to the Earth. When we send our 3rd-Dimensional instruments to Mars or Venus, the only thing we see is the densest residue of matter. We come to the erroneous conclusion that Life may have existed on those planets millions of years ago, but that they could not sustain Life now. In reality, the other 143 planets in the system of Alpha and Omega are teaming with Life. It is just that we cannot see them, because they are vibrating in the

4th Dimension at frequencies beyond our physical sight.

The Sons and Daughters of God evolving on these planets are very aware of the sacrifice the people of Earth made to save their sisters and brothers. They are eternally grateful to us, and they are helping us in monumental ways to succeed with our experiment. Their UFOs pass easily between dimensions, bringing guidance and assistance to Earth in ways we cannot perceive. When the UFOs pass from the 3rd Dimension into the 4th Dimension, they disappear from our physical sight. This is why UFOs seem so illusive.

## EMBODIMENT OF THE FALLEN SOULS

The Beings of Light said that the greatest sacrifice ever made by the Sons and Daughters of God was when the women of Earth volunteered to allow the contaminated souls from the other planets to embody on Earth through their physical bodies. The Christ Selves and the Body Elementals of the women who would be the mothers of these incoming souls, prepared their etheric, mental, emotional, and physical bodies for over 100 years to be able to withstand the discordant vibrations that these souls were obligated to bring with them into embodiment.

When everything was in place, the fallen souls were conceived by the millions on planet Earth. The first influx of these souls embodied on the continent of Lemuria. Lemuria, or Mu as it is sometimes called, was an enormous landmass that used to exist in the Pacific Ocean. The Hawaiian Islands, Indonesia, the islands of the South Pacific, Australia, and New Zealand were at one time part of this huge continent.

In the beginning, the experiment seemed to be working. The

people of Earth flooded these incoming souls with love and compassion. We gently guided them in the right direction, and taught them how to transmute their misqualified thoughts and feelings with the Violet Flame of God's Infinite Perfection. When the fallen souls were children, only a small amount of the energy associated with their human miscreations was returned to them at a time. These patterns of imperfection were manageable and easily transmuted back into Light. Even though the people of Earth were not familiar with these human miscreations, we just viewed the patterns as objective observers. We were not tempted to interact with them in any way.

When the fallen souls reached maturity, however, things dramatically changed. The Law of the Circle dictated that greater amounts of their misqualified energy must be returned to them, so that they could fulfill their karmic liabilities. It was time for these souls to experience the results of their past thoughts, feelings, words, and actions. It was time for them to transmute these human miscreations back into Light.

This facet of the plan resulted in overwhelming amounts of negative energy being projected into the physical plane. The sheer magnitude of these patterns of imperfection shocked and dismayed the people of Earth. We had never experienced anything like the pain and suffering involved with these human miscreations, and we had no idea how to help these souls transcend such gross and oppressive mutations of their Lifeforce.

When this negativity began to reflect on the Elemental Kingdom, the fallen souls started to experience aging and disease. The environment around them began to show signs of deterioration and decay. The people of Earth had never witnessed anything like this, and we became afraid and confused.

In the midst of our fear and confusion, we became curious

about the negativity that was starting to manifest around the fallen souls. We began interacting with the distorted patterns that were responsible for causing so much pain and suffering. Once we chose to deliberately become involved with this energy, *the game plan on Earth changed.* By making the free-will decision to interact with these human miscreations, we willingly partook of the tree of knowledge of good and evil.

In the allegory of Adam and Eve, it is said that Eve was enticed by the serpent to eat the apple in the Garden of Eden. Consequently, women have been blamed for Humanity's fall from Grace. This misinterpretation has wreaked havoc in the lives of women for aeons of time. The real reason it is said that Eve ate the apple is because it was the feminine aspect of love and compassion within us that reached out to our fallen sisters and brothers. It was our love that inspired us to attempt this unique experiment. Our love is the Divine Essence of our Mother God.

Partaking of the tree of knowledge of good and evil had nothing to do with being a man or a woman. It was the feminine aspect of love within *all* of the people on Earth that motivated us to appeal to Alpha and Omega on behalf of the fallen souls in this system. It was our love that prompted us to invite our fallen sisters and brothers to Earth. This selfless act of love is what opened the door for human miscreations to be brought to Earth for the very first time.

In the allegory of Adam and Eve it is said that once Eve partook of the tree of knowledge of good and evil, both she and Adam were banished from the Garden of Eden. They began to experience fear, pain, and suffering for the first time. Inclement weather conditions began to manifest on Earth causing famine, pestilence, lack, and limitation of all kinds. This part of the allegory depicts what actually took place once the people of Earth willingly partook of the tree of knowledge of good and evil. These catastrophic changes occurred when our negative thoughts and feelings were projected onto the Elemental Kingdom in the Garden of Eden. This was the catalyst for our fall from Grace.

## OUR FALL FROM GRACE

Even though we got into this painful situation out of the greatest act of compassion and love the Children of God had ever demonstrated for our sisters and brothers, we were still accountable for our free-will choices.

The Law of the Circle is accurate to the letter, and we are all subject to this Universal Law. It does not matter if we know about the Law of the Circle or if we comprehend how it affects our lives. It does not even matter whether or not we believe that the Law of the Circle exists. We are subject to it just the same.

As Children of God, we are responsible for how we choose to use every atomic and subatomic particle and wave of our Lifeforce. With every thought, feeling, word, or action we are cocreating patterns that are either adding to the Light of the world or to the shadows. Depending on the frequency of vibration we send forth, our cocreations will either be a blessing or cause a problem for ourselves and all Life on this planet.

The Law of the Circle mandates that we experience everything we create through our thoughts, feelings, words, and actions. This is how we learn to become cocreators with our Father-Mother God. The Law of the Circle will eventually return to us every electron of Lifeforce that we have ever sent forth. This process allows us to experience what we have created through our free-will choices, and it gives us the opportunity to transmute our miscreations back into Light.

It matters not whether we deliberately or inadvertently created the patterns manifesting in our lives. The Law of the Circle is neutral. There is no judgment. Our energy just returns to us, charged with whatever frequency we sent forth. If our returning energy is vibrating with a positive frequency, it brings good things into our lives and blesses us with our positive cocreations on its return journey back to the Source. If the frequency of vibration is negative, our returning energy brings challenging circumstances into our lives that give us the opportunity to experience and transmute our human miscreations.

It is important to understand that our Lifeforce cannot return to the Source unless it is vibrating at the same or a higher frequency than our Christ Self originally received from our Father-Mother God. This means that our negative energy and our human miscreations cannot return to the Source. These patterns of imperfection must remain in our energy field until we transmute them back into Light. It was the accumulation of this heavy, negative energy that perpetuated our fall from Grace and wreaked havoc in the lives of all of the Children of God evolving on this planet.

Once the people of Earth began using our Lifeforce to cocreate patterns of imperfection, which we had learned from the fallen souls, our descent into chaos was inevitable. The negative energy from our miscreations began to fill the atmosphere around us. The discordant frequency of this energy caused our Earthly bodies to became denser and denser. We began experiencing aging, degeneration, disease, and pain for the first time.

Our human miscreations were projected onto the Elemental Kingdom. This caused these selfless servants of Humanity to reflect decay and degeneration. The Elementals had always sustained us with abundant food, air, water, clothing, and shelter, but as our miscreations accumulated around the Earth, inclement weather conditions began to manifest in the Garden of Eden. We started experiencing droughts and floods, which disrupted the balance, causing famines, plagues, and pestilence.

With this turn of events, the Children of Earth began experiencing lack and limitation for the first time. We became concerned that we were not going to have enough of the things we needed for our survival. We started hoarding the necessities of life and taking things away from our sisters and brothers. These actions accelerated our descent into chaos. We became more anxious and less trusting, which compelled us to separate into family clans in order to protect ourselves from each other. As time passed, our fear intensified and our pain become more excruciating. We forgot about our interdependence and the Oneness of Life. Day by day, we fell further into the abyss of separation and fear.

The overwhelming pain and suffering we were cocreating for ourselves was a new experience for us. We were afraid, and we had no idea how to cope with what was happening in our lives. We were so buried in our self-inflicted strife that we could not raise our heads above the mud puddle of our miscreations. This prevented us from perceiving viable solutions to our problems. All we wanted to do was make the pain stop.

We knew that our Heart Chakra was the portal through which our feelings were expressed in the physical plane. We thought that maybe if we blocked this portal, the pain would stop. So the Children of Earth, in a desperate attempt to stop our pain, decided to close our Heart Chakras.

The Beings of Light revealed that when we closed our Heart Chakras, we blocked the portal through which our Mother God's Love entered the physical plane of Earth. This catastrophic occurrence forced our Mother God to withdraw her Love to a mere trickle of its original intensity. This created monumental problems that catapulted the Earth and all her Life into a downward spiral of darkness, pain, and suffering.

## THE WITHDRAWAL OF
## OUR MOTHER GOD'S LOVE

Once we closed our Heart Chakras, the infinitesimal amount of Divine Love our Mother God was able to project through our right-brain hemispheres, was barely enough to sustain brain consciousness. This caused our right brains to became almost dormant. When that occurred, the Blue Flame of Power from our Father God and the Pink Flame of Love from our Mother God no longer merged into the perfectly balanced Violet Flame of God's Infinite Perfection.

Our Father-Mother God's balanced Violet Flame was the catalyst that activated our spiritual brain centers and opened our Crown Chakras. Without the support of the Violet Flame, our spiritual brain centers began to atrophy. This forced our Crown Chakras to close, which prevented our Christ Selves from staying connected to the higher aspects of our own Divinity and the Company of Heaven. We were no longer able to maintain Christ Consciousness.

When our Christ Selves lost conscious awareness of the other aspects of our Divinity and the Company of Heaven, we started to perceive the physical plane as our only reality. We came to the distorted conclusion that our physical body is all that we are and that the gratification of our physical senses is our purpose and reason for being. As we plodded through our Earthly existence making choices that took us further into separation and darkness, we developed a fear-based alter ego. This fragmented aspect of our personality is known as our *human ego*. Our human egos usurped the control our Christ Selves had over our Earthly bodies.

Without the balance of our Mother God's Love, we began abusing our masculine power. We made power-oriented decisions that did not take into consideration how our choices would affect other people, or if they reflected a reverence for Life. When we were in male bodies we abused our power by being violent and aggressive. When we were in female bodies, we abused our power by suppressing it and allowing ourselves to be dominated and oppressed. The more we abused our power, the deeper we fell into the abyss of our human miscreations. As time went on, our plight became much worse.

In an attempt to prevent us from being buried in negative energy, our 4th-Dimensional Solar Christ Presence withdrew a major portion of the Lifeforce it was sending to our 3rd-Dimensional Christ Self. This sad, but merciful, act reduced our Christ Self to a mere fraction of its original stature. Instead of a full-grown Being, through which our human ego could misqualify tons of our Lifeforce, our Christ Self and our Immortal Victorious Threefold Flame became a tiny *spark of Divinity* in our heart. When this happened, the shaft of Light that flowed through our Chakra System was reduced to a small stream of Light—what we now refer to as our *silver cord.*

Even though we were misqualifying smaller amounts of our Lifeforce, when our fear-based human ego gained dominion of our thoughts, feelings, words, and actions, things got progressively worse. Since our human ego believed that its sole purpose was to gratify our physical senses, it decided that whatever it needed to do to accomplish that goal would be just fine. This self-serving decision gave our ego permission to lie, cheat, steal, and kill to get whatever it wanted. These destructive behavior patterns catapulted us further into darkness and greatly amplified our pain and suffering.

We fell deeper and deeper into frequencies of lack and limitation. This caused the twelve Solar Strands of DNA, which our Father-Mother God gave to us with the intent of keeping us connected to the Twelve Solar Aspects of Deity, to short circuit. Our twelve strands of DNA deteriorated into a double-helix, which barely contained enough of our genetic messenger codes to keep us alive in the 3rd Dimension. When this happened, our Body Elemental was no longer able to keep our Elemental Vortices open. This prevented our etheric, mental, emotional, and physical bodies from holding the frequency of our Christ Self's Light Body. Our bodies began to age and deteriorate causing disease and all kinds of physical ailments. Our life expectancy plummeted to a fraction of what it was originally.

When our DNA short circuited, our brain capacity deteriorated even further to a mere ten percent of its original potential. This caused us to fall to a caveman's level of consciousness. The Neanderthal's and Troglodyte's mental and physical capacities reflect the level of consciousness to which the Children of Earth fell. This is not the level from which the Human Race originally evolved, as our scientists believe. It is only because our bones became so very dense that they lasted for millions of years and our archaeologists were able to find them. Prior to that, our Earthly bodies were much more rarified. No trace of those vehicles exists now.

In spite of our loving intentions, the Children of Earth ended up in the very situation that we were striving so courageously to prevent our fallen sisters and brothers from having to experience.

Alpha and Omega and all of the Beings of Light associated with this Solar System were well aware of the tragedy occurring on Earth. They knew that we had gotten ourselves into this painful situation by trying to keep our sisters and brothers from suffering the fate of being left behind during the Shift of the Ages. Due to this unprecedented demonstration of Divine Love, no one was willing to give up on us.

Alpha and Omega appealed to our Father-Mother God and asked for Divine Intervention to help the Children of Earth reverse our descent into chaos and confusion. The situation was evaluated, and a plan was set into motion. The goal was for the Company of Heaven to help us reverse the adverse effects of the fall. This had to be done without interfering with our free will or the learning experiences we had cocreated after partaking of the tree of knowledge of good and evil.

# CHAPTER FIVE

# REVERSING THE ADVERSE EFFECTS OF THE FALL

For literally millions of years the Beings of Light from the Realms of Illumined Truth have been implementing various plans to try to extricate Humanity from the adverse effects of our fall from Grace.

By the time we reached the caveman level of consciousness, our human ego had taken complete control of our Earthly bodies. Our Christ Self and our Immortal Victorious Threefold Flame were just a spark of Divinity in our heart. The clamor and noise from the chaos we had created prevented us from hearing any guidance our Christ Self was trying to give us. In fact, our Christ Self became what we call *the still small voice within*.

Even though our brain capacity was greatly diminished, we still had conscious awareness of our previous lifetimes. We remembered who our enemies were, and the atrocities our human egos had inflicted upon each other. Each time we reincarnated, we just picked up where we left off. We continued our battles and our fear-based, hate-filled behavior patterns. This intensified the pain and suffering not only for ourselves but for all Life on this planet.

Lifetime after lifetime, our negative energy became darker and more oppressive as it amassed around us. This seething forcefield of our human miscreations formed a sea of negativity that eventually enveloped the Earth. This is the *psychic-astral plane*, also known as the *veil of illusion* or the *veil of maya*. This accumulation of Humanity's negative thoughts, feelings, words, and actions is where the concept of *hell* came from.

People who have had a near-death experience consistently

report that they passed through a *dark tunnel* as they moved toward the Light. This phenomenon is happening to people regardless of their religious beliefs, education, culture, socioeconomic status, or any other factor that categorizes people and their experiences. The dark tunnel they pass through is the psychic-astral plane.

When we die, we are vibrating at a frequency that reflects the sum total of our thoughts, feelings, words, and actions. If our frequency is very discordant, instead of passing through the dark tunnel into the Light we may get pulled into a like vibration in the psychic-astral plane. This is never our Divine Plan, and it is not the intent of our Father-Mother God for us to be trapped in this forcefield of human miscreations. The Will of God is always for every Son and Daughter to have the opportunity to move forward in the Light.

As soon as we are pulled into the psychic-astral plane, Angels are sent to inform us that we have been drawn into that humanly created forcefield of chaos by mistake. The Angels tell us that we are not supposed to be there, and they ask us to come with them. They volunteer to escort us to the schools in the inner planes, so we can prepare for the next phase of our evolutionary process.

The Angels will not interfere with our free will, and they will not force us to go with them. Sometimes the souls trapped in the psychic-astral plane are so mischievous or so confused that they do not want to move into the Light. They realize that they can have a degree of access to the physical plane from that frequency of chaos, so they choose to remain there. These are the souls we perceive as ghosts or Earthbound spirits. Even though the Angels keep returning to offer the trapped souls the opportunity to move into the Light, they have the free will to refuse. They can remain in the psychic-astral plane for aeons of time if they choose to do so.

We are always a sum total of everything we have ever thought, felt, said, or done, so when mischievous souls choose to remain in the psychic-astral plane for a very long time, they can become extremely negative individuals. This is where the concept of Satan or demons came from. We must remember that these are just Children of God who have lost their way. They have no power over the Light, and the only influence they have in our lives is what we give to them through the power of our attention. The purpose of our invincible pillar of Light, which surrounds us and extends from the Heart of God into the center of the Earth, is to prevent these fallen sisters and brothers from distracting us or interfering in our lives in any way.

Once Humanity realized that very negative souls could end up in the psychic-astral plane, we started developing the concept of hell. We looked at this sea of negativity and came to the erroneous conclusion that God must have created this place to punish bad people. As the concept of a hell grew in our minds, the world religions decided to use that belief to make people behave in ways that would keep them aligned with the rules of the particular religion. The threat of an eternal hell, fire, and damnation inflicted on Humanity by a wrathful God, seemed like a good motivator for our recalcitrant human egos.

Now that the Beings of Light have reminded us of the Divine Truth that our Father-Mother God are pure Love, these distorted beliefs are exposed for the sacrilege they are. For example, if you knew a father who sent his child to a place to be burned and tortured because the child could not comprehend what the father was trying to teach him, you would call the police and have that father arrested. Even as confused and distorted as Humanity's perception often is at this time, we know it is wrong for a father to have his child tortured and burned for any reason. We would put that father on trial, and a jury would convict him of being a psychopath. Then we would either put him in a mental institution, or we would sentence him to jail for a very long time.

Imagine! This is what some religions are saying God will do to a person who does not grasp the concept of accepting Jesus as his or her personal savior. This is also what many of the world religions are saying God will do to us for a multitude of other so-called sins, or if we do not accept the tenets of their particular religion. This belief is the antithesis of who our Father-Mother God are. For us to say that our Beloved God Parents would do this to their Children is the epitome of what the word "blasphemy" means.

Our Father-Mother God do not release one electron of precious Life energy that is vibrating at a frequency less than pure Divine Love. Every painful experience we are going through is the result of our own thoughts and feelings returning to us through the Law of the Circle. When we remember that we have had hundreds or maybe even thousands of lifetimes, and that at any given moment our lives are reflecting the sum total of everything we have ever created with our thoughts, feelings, words, and actions, we begin to get a glimpse of how we could be in the situations we are in, both good and bad. Whatever it is that we are experiencing could be the result of lessons we created in this lifetime, or it might be lessons we created in another time frame or dimension. We have gone through the gamut of experiences, and we have all probably been and done everything.

It does not matter if we created the situations we are going through intentionally or inadvertently. Either way, what is happening in our lives is the result of our free-will choices and how we expressed our thoughts and feelings during our various Earthly sojourns. This is true for everything we are experiencing, both the wonderful things and the challenging things.

What does matter is that we realize we are not going through our challenges because we are evil, worthless sinners being punished by a jealous, wrathful God. Neither are we just innocent victims who are going through these challenges by happenstance for no rhyme or reason. We are going through our experiences because we are learning to become cocreators with our Father-Mother God. In order for us to learn the lessons of cocreation, we must experience the results of what we are creating. It is just that simple.

The Beings of Light are not giving us this information to make us feel guilty or ashamed about the things we have done in the past. Quite the contrary, they are reminding us of these Truths to empower us and to inspire us to take charge of our lives. They want us to know that we are not the victims of circumstance. We are beloved Children of God, and we are powerful beyond our knowing. We have cocreated the present reality on Earth, so if we do not like the way things are going, we can change them. We have the absolute ability to not only transmute our human miscreations back into Light, but to cocreate the perfection of Heaven on Earth. That is precisely why these experiences are returning to us in the first place through the Law of the Circle.

Even though it has taken hundreds or thousands of lifetimes for us to get into the mess we are in on this planet, it is not going to take anywhere near that length of time for us to turn things around. Light is infinitely more powerful than the fragmented, fear-based thoughts and feelings of our human egos. In fact, a small group of people focusing intensely on the Light can transmute the misqualified thoughts and feelings of hundreds of thousands of people. With that same level of dedication, we can transmute hundreds of lifetimes worth of our own misqualified energy in a very short time. This is what the phrase *"in the twinkling of an eye"* is all about.

# THE BAND OF FORGETFULNESS

As time progressed, it became clear to the Company of Heaven that Humanity was in a catastrophic tailspin. It seemed as though we would need some kind of Divine Intervention in order to extricate ourselves from our dire situation. Once again an appeal was made to Alpha and Omega for assistance.

Alpha and Omega agreed that the conscious awareness we had of all of the negative experiences from our previous lifetimes was making it very difficult for us to move forward. Our grudges and our thoughts of revenge overwhelmed any desire we may have had to heal our relationships. To try and remedy this problem, permission was granted for a *Band of Forgetfulness* to be placed around the conscious mind of every incarnating soul. We would be allowed to remember all of our experiences when we were in the schools in the inner planes between embodiments, but the Band of Forgetfulness would prevent us from remembering any previous lives while we were reincarnated on Earth.

The intent of this facet of the experiment was for us to have a fresh start each lifetime with our relationships. Even though we would be with the people we needed to work out our karmic liabilities with, we would not remember the specifics of our past relationships. The hope was that this would enable us to create positive interactions that would heal the negativity we had created in the past.

The Band of Forgetfulness helped to a degree, but it created a whole new series of problems. Since we had no knowledge of the things we had done in our previous lifetimes, we had no explanation as to why we were going through such challenging situations. When a baby was born into poverty or some other difficult condition, it seemed as though a perfectly innocent child was suffering without cause. We did not remember that the baby was an incoming soul who had experienced many previous lives, and that the soul was going through the lessons he or she had previously created in order to learn how to become a cocreator with our Father-Mother God.

When we tried to figure out why an innocent child would be suffering in such a way, we came up with a lot of distorted answers. We blamed Eve for eating the apple from the tree of knowledge of good and evil. We blamed the situation on punishment from a wrathful, vengeful God. We blamed ourselves for being worthless sinners and worms in the dust. We blamed it on happenstance or coincidence. And most discouraging, we accepted the lie that it was, of all things, God's Will. All of these beliefs intensified the separation we perceived between our Father-Mother God and ourselves. Eventually, we came to the devastating conclusion that we were victims, and that we were powerless to change our circumstances.

Even when we were in the greatest depths of our fall from Grace, the Company of Heaven was not willing to give up on us. As we struggled through our humanly created pain and suffering, plan after plan was set into motion to try and help us. Each plan was an attempt to get us to lift our heads above the chaos, so we could perceive the Light once again. Due to our free will and the tenacious resistance of our human egos, the best laid plans of the Beings of Light had varying degrees of success and failure.

## OUTSIDE   INTERFERENCE

Once we accepted the illusion that we were powerless, our human egos became susceptible to outside influences. Throughout history there have been legends about interference from the fallen Children of God who came to Earth from outside of the Solar System of Alpha and Omega. This seemed so outrageous that we usually discounted these stories as myths. Now the Company of Heaven is confirming that aeons ago some interference did occur. This information is being shared very briefly at this time to help us understand what we have been through and how very far we have come on our journey back to God.

After we came to the erroneous conclusion that we were powerless, some of our fallen sisters and brothers from other systems realized our vulnerability and decided to take advantage of the opportunity. They even went so far as to procreate with the Children of Earth in an attempt to perpetuate their nefarious plans. The fragmented state of our DNA made our genetic codings malleable. This allowed the fallen souls to change our DNA in ways that enabled them to manipulate us.

The Company of Heaven revealed that the modifications made in our DNA by these souls changed the Earth from a school of cocreation and empowerment, to a school of duality and separation. The goal was to prevent us from remembering that we are Children of God. They knew that if we became aware of our Divine Heritage, and if we remembered that all that our Father-Mother God have is ours, they would not be able to manipulate or control us. Their malevolent plan seemed to succeed and took us off course for a very long time, but the Beings of Light did not give up. They kept monitoring our situation, looking for opportunities that would allow them to intervene without interfering with our free will.

# REINFORCEMENTS

Alpha and Omega and the Beings of Light serving the Earth were well aware of how entrapped we were allowing ourselves to become. They wanted to do something to try to extricate us from the paralyzing grip of these outside influences. In a selfless act of Divine Love, many of our sisters and brothers from the other planets in our Solar System volunteered to embody on Earth. The hope was that when the 12 Solar Strands of their DNA were intermingled with the manipulated DNA of the Children of Earth, the negative affects of our manipulated DNA would be reversed. The Children of Earth could then release the lessons of separation and duality and reclaim our Divine Mission of becoming cocreators with our Father-Mother God. This would allow us to move forward a quantum leap in our evolutionary process.

Unfortunately, the fallen souls from the other systems had different plans. They were not willing to give up control of the Earth so easily. Their resistance manifested as a struggle of epic proportions, which persisted on this planet for millennia. That ongoing battle resulted in the sinking of Lemuria and eventually the sinking of Atlantis, a massive continent in the Atlantic Ocean. But the Light of God is infinitely more powerful than darkness, so in spite of all of the resistance, little-by-little the Light began returning to Earth. With that renewed glimmer of hope, the Company of Heaven redoubled their efforts, and plans for the salvation of Humanity were initiated once again in earnest.

# CHAPTER SIX

# THE PRECESSION OF
# THE EQUINOXES

The Precession of the Equinoxes is a celestial event that determines the various cycles we refer to as *Ages*. This event also involves the period of time known as the *New Age*. Currently there is a lot of fear-based misinformation and disinformation about the term "New Age." Whenever there is new information coming to the forefront that challenges our present belief system, our first response is to become suspicious and afraid. Once we let go of our fear and open our hearts and minds, we are able to perceive things in a higher Light with greater clarity.

Let me briefly share with you what a New Age really is. A New Age is not a new religion, a movement, a philosophy, or the work of the devil as some are professing. The dawn of a New Age is nothing more than a span of time. It involves the natural cycles of the Precession of the Equinoxes, which the Earth has gone through since her inception.

As our Earth revolves on her axis every 24 hours, we experience a new day. As she orbits around the Sun every 365 and 1/4 days, we experience a new year. On the orbit around the Sun, the Earth passes through the forcefields of the 12 natural constellations, which form our zodiac. During this annual orbit, the Earth and all Life evolving upon her are held in the Light and influence of these constellations for 28 to 31 days. These are our familiar Sun cycles: Capricorn, Aquarius, Pisces, et cetera. Each of these constellations pulsates with one of the Twelve Solar Aspects of Deity. During the time we are held in the forcefield of each Sun cycle, the Earth is bathed with the Divine Qualities of that particular Solar Aspect of Deity.

| | |
|---|---|
| Capricorn - | the 8th Solar Aspect of Deity |
| Aquarius - | the 7th Solar Aspect of Deity |
| Pisces - | the 6th Solar Aspect of Deity |
| Aries - | the 5th Solar Aspect of Deity |
| Taurus - | the 4th Solar Aspect of Deity |
| Gemini - | the 3rd Solar Aspect of Deity |
| Cancer - | the 2nd Solar Aspect of Deity |
| Leo - | the 1st Solar Aspect of Deity |
| Virgo - | the 12th Solar Aspect of Deity |
| Libra - | the 11th Solar Aspect of Deity |
| Scorpio - | the 10th Solar Aspect of Deity |
| Sagittarius- | the 9th Solar Aspect of Deity |

In addition to these very obvious time frames, the Earth is part of a much larger celestial event that is called the Precession of the Equinoxes. This precession is created by the wobble the Earth makes due to the slanted position of the axis. This is a counterclockwise rotation that moves the Earth very slowly through the influence of the 12 constellations. It takes approximately 26,000 years for the Earth to complete one rotation in the Precession of the Equinoxes.

The Earth's movement in this precession is measured at the point where the Sun passes the equator on the Vernal Equinox each year. This point moves about 52 seconds per year, so it takes about 72 years for the Earth to move one degree in this rotation. During this precession, the Earth is held in the forcefield and bathed with the Solar Aspect of Deity of each constellation for approximately 30 degrees, or 2,000 plus a few years. These 2,000-year cycles are what we call Ages.

The dawn of a New Age is a period of time that lasts between 150 and 300 years. It is a window of opportunity during the Precession of the Equinoxes when the energies from the Solar Aspect of Deity of the constellation we are leaving begin to ebb, and the energies from the Solar Aspect of Deity of the constellation we are moving into have not yet taken hold. It is during this lull of energy that our Father-Mother God and the Company of Heaven evaluate our progress and determine what information and what lessons would be most beneficial for our spiritual growth in the dawning New Age.

Prior to the fall, we made tremendous progress during each Age. We easily learned the lessons associated with the Solar Aspect of Deity we were under the influence of at the time. Our cocreations were positive, and they were a blessing to us and to all Life. The things we experienced through the Law of the Circle were always a joy and filled with Light.

When the dawn of each New Age arrived, it was easy for our God Parents and the Company of Heaven to determine the next level of sacred knowledge that we would need to help us with our lessons of cocreation. This new information filtered down through the higher aspects of our Divinity into our conscious minds. Since we were aware of who we are and our purpose and reason for being, our Christ Self accepted this new information with enthusiasm and gratitude.

After the fall, the lessons we were given during the dawn of each New Age changed dramatically. Once we began misqualifying our Lifeforce, we were no longer coming to Earth with the sole purpose of progressing with our joy-filled lessons of becoming cocreators. We were coming to Earth to transmute the distorted patterns we had created through the misuse of our thoughts and feelings in our previous lives.

Without the balance of our Mother God's Love, our perception was very distorted. We forgot about the Oneness of all Life, and we kept abusing our power. Each lifetime we ended up creating more negativity for ourselves and the planet. Lifetime after lifetime we descended further into darkness and chaos. During this time the windows of opportunity provided by the dawning New Ages had very little influence in changing our direction. We were so buried in the oppressive energy of our human miscreation that we were not able to perceive the guidance from On High that was trying to filter into our conscious minds. It seemed as though we were never going to be able to stop our downward spiral, but the Company of Heaven would not give up on us.

The sinking of the final portion of the landmass of Atlantis occurred about 12,000 years ago. That catastrophic event completed the purging of massive amounts of Humanity's collective negative energy. The submerging of Lemuria and Atlantis, which took place over tens of thousands of years, purged the Earth of most of the interference we were receiving from outside sources. The vast majority of fallen souls trapped in the psychic-astral plane were released and taken to schools in the inner planes where they could complete their lessons and learn how to move forward in the Light.

The dense veil of illusion that had blocked God's Light from the Earth for millions of years became much more rarified. Our sisters and brothers who had volunteered to embody on Earth from the other planets in the system of Alpha and Omega, were at long last able to pierce through the veil and to raise their consciousness into the Realms of Light.

After aeons  of struggling with the forces of imbalance that were striving to keep us entrapped in separation and duality, the Children of Earth began to make some progress. Since Light is infinitely more powerful than darkness, it did not take many awakened people to make a profound difference in the amount of Divine Light that was finally reaching the Earth. This shift allowed our Father-Mother God and the Company of Heaven to initiate new and powerful plans to assist the Children of Earth during the dawning of the various New Ages.

Several Ages ago, during the window of opportunity for the New Age, Alpha and Omega evaluated the progress we were making on Earth. It became clear that the Light of God was finally returning to this planet. There were even a few souls who had awakened enough to complete their lessons of becoming cocreators. When their lessons were finished these souls Ascended into the 4th Dimension. Their Christ Self became one with their 4th-Dimensional Solar Christ Presence, and they began the next phase of their evolutionary process.

The human egos of the unawakened people on Earth were oblivious to what was taking place with our sisters and brothers who were completing their lessons of cocreation. We had no concept of what it meant to Ascend into the higher schools of learning. We did not realize that it was even possible to raise our consciousness, so we just plodded along in our mundane lives with no thought or awareness that we could improve our Earthly plight.

Alpha and Omega decided that the greatest need of the hour was for unawakened Humanity to have an example that we could clearly see of our Divine Potential. Since our awakened sisters and brothers Ascended into the 4th Dimension when their lessons were complete, we could no longer see them. We had no idea what it was like to have an Ascended Master's awakened consciousness.

Alpha and Omega thought that if our Ascended sisters and brothers would remain within the frequency of our physical sight after they reached their awakened consciousness, we could see how advanced they were. Then, hopefully, we would be inspired to emulate their positive behavior. Alpha and Omega asked for volunteers to implement this experiment for the dawning New Age. Many of our Ascended sisters and brothers agreed to lower their frequency of vibration to remain within the physical sight of the unawakened Children of Earth.

As time passed we did become aware of how advanced these Ascended souls were. We saw that through the positive use of their thoughts and feelings, they were able to manifest wonderful things in their lives and create experiences of harmony and joy that we had not experienced for aeons of time. As they lived their lives in their Ascended state of consciousness, we were in awe over what appeared to be miracles. It never occurred to us that these Beings were just demonstrating our own human potential.

We were so beaten down by our victim consciousness that we assumed these Beings were powerful gods and goddesses who had come to save us. We started worshiping them and expecting them to do for us the very things they were trying to teach us that we could do for ourselves. After a period of time, it became clear to the Company of Heaven that this experiment was not working. The Ascended Beings were becoming a distraction for Humanity instead of an inspiration. As long as we were giving our power away and expecting someone outside of ourselves to save us, we were not going to progress. With this realization, Alpha and Omega sounded a Cosmic Tone, and the Ascended Beings raised their vibrations back into the frequencies of the 4th Dimension.

For all intents and purposes our Ascended sisters and brothers just disappeared from the face of the Earth. This caused a great deal of fear and confusion for the unawakened souls. We had no idea what happened to the Beings we considered gods and goddesses. In desperation we tried to recreate them by building statues and making replicas of them that we could worship. We devised outlandish stories and wove our distorted perceptions and desires into these tales. We made the gods and goddesses superhuman Beings, and we continued giving our power away to the idols we had built in their honor.

This was the period we refer to historically as the time of Greek Mythology. Since there was no evidence of the Ascended Beings left behind in the 3rd Dimension, we started to doubt that such advanced souls ever walked the Earth. The stories we concocted were so fragmented and so bizarre that as time passed, not only the stories but also the Ascended Beings we thought of as gods and goddesses were classified as myths.

During the dawn of the next New Age, our Father-Mother God and the Company of Heaven once again evaluated the greatest need of the hour for the Children of Earth. At that time our human egos still believed that the 3rd Dimension was the only reality. Even though the psychic-astral plane was not nearly as dense as it once was, it still blocked a lot of God's Light from the Earth. We were oblivious to the Realms of Illumined Truth, and the masses of Humanity did not know it was possible to raise our consciousness above the pain and suffering we had created.

It was determined by the Beings of Light that what Humanity needed the most for the dawning New Age was a method of raising our consciousness above the chaos of our human miscreations. We needed to pierce through the psychic-astral plane and enter the Realms of Illumined Truth to perceive the Light of God once again. In order to accomplish this facet of the Divine Plan, the teachings of the many disciplines involving meditation, breathing exercises, physical movement, chanting, mantras, and the other teachings we now classify as Eastern philosophies or religions began to flow into the conscious minds of Humanity.

The souls who were receptive to these teachings began to absorb this knowledge and apply these practices in their daily lives. The various meditation disciplines allowed people to lift up in consciousness and to pierce through the psychic-astral plane. They entered the Realms of Light, and they began to remember some of their Divine Potential. They learned how to breathe the Light of God into the physical plane on the Holy Breath, which greatly added to the Light of the world. This sacred knowledge filtered into the conscious minds of Humanity throughout that Age. During that time a great deal of progress was made, but there were still some serious problems.

During the dawn of the next New Age another evaluation was made by our Father-Mother God and the Company of Heaven. Things were indeed better, but Humanity was still worshiping the various gods and goddesses. Our human egos were power-oriented and self-obsessed, so separation and duality were all we remembered on a conscious level. We could not comprehend the Oneness of our Father-Mother God, so we continued to think of God as fragmented. We worshiped the idols we built of the various gods and goddesses, and we waited for them to come and save us.

It was clear to Alpha and Omega that the Children of Earth needed to be reminded of the One God. We needed to stop worshiping false idols, and we needed to know that we are all Children of God. To accomplish this goal, monotheism and the sacred doctrine we now call Judaism began filtering into our conscious minds. The Children of Earth who were receptive to these teaching began absorbing this sacred knowledge and applying it to their lives. They learned to stop worshiping false idols. They realized that there is just One God, and that we are all God's Children. During that Age the Children of Earth moved a little further into the Light, but due to the manipulation of our fear-based human egos, we had some misperceptions that continued to slow our progress.

Because of the Band of Forgetfulness, we could not understand why the Children of God were going through so much pain and suffering. We came to the conclusion that we must be very bad, and that God was angry with us. We developed the belief that God was wrathful and vengeful. We blamed all of our woes on the fact that we were being punished because we are worthless sinners and worms in the dust. We learned to fear God, and we tried to do whatever was necessary to avoid God's wrath. Since we are cocreating this reality, and since we become who we believe we are, these beliefs only perpetuated our pain and suffering. Our feelings of inadequacy perpetuated the belief that someone outside of ourselves would have to come and save us.

It was certainly not the intent of the sacred teachings of that Age to instill such fear in the Children of Earth, but fear was the state of mind that allowed our human egos to manipulate us most effectively. This fragmented aspect of our personality did whatever it could to keep us controlled through fear.

When it was time for the dawn of the next New Age another evaluation was made by our Father-Mother God and the Company of Heaven. This was the dawn of the Piscean Age, which occurred a little over 2,000 years ago. The Children of Earth were becoming aware that there is only One God— the Cosmic I AM—All That Is, and that even though we are very flawed, we are somehow all Children of God. We had lost the awareness of our Mother God long ago, so it did not occur to us that this all-encompassing Presence of God was both masculine and feminine. We assumed that the One God was male, and we accepted without question that we had a single parent, a Father God.

It was clear to Alpha and Omega that the time had arrived for the Children of Earth to reclaim our Divine Birthright as Sons and Daughters of God. We needed to take our power back from our human egos, and we needed to give our Christ Selves dominion of our lives. There was only one way to accomplish that goal. Our Christ Selves could not regain control of our Earthly bodies without the balance of our Mother God's Love.

In order to reverse the adverse affects of our fall from Grace, we would have to open our Heart Chakras and balance our Mother God's Flame of Divine Love within the Immortal Victorious Threefold Flame in our hearts. Only then could our right- and left-brain hemispheres become balanced, and our spiritual brain centers reactivated with the Violet Flame of God's Infinite Perfection.

The return of our Mother God was the only way our Crown Chakras could open to full breadth, so we could regain Christ Consciousness. Only then could our Christ Selves take back the power that had been usurped by our human egos, and regain full dominion of our Earthly bodies. This would be the most ambitious undertaking since the initial impulse of our fall from Grace. The entire Company of Heaven was standing in readiness to help with this holy endeavor.

A Divine Plan was set into motion, and a Beloved Son and Daughter of God were summoned from the Great Silence. These precious Beings are Twin Flames who had been in the Great Silence for a very long time learning how to anchor the archetypes for the return of our Mother God, and Humanity's return to Christ Consciousness. They are the ones we know as Jesus the Christ and Mary Magdalene. These selfless Beings of Light volunteered to embody on Planet Earth to demonstrate to the Children of God evolving here the reality of our Mother God, and the pathway back to Christ Consciousness. A critical facet of their Divine Mission was to model the path of Oneness and Divine Love through Christ Consciousness, which is the *only* way back to the Heart of God.

Jesus and Mary Magdalene knew that because of Humanity's ingrained belief in the patriarchal authority of a single Father God, Mary's role would initially be as a silent partner. Her part of the Divine Plan was cloaked in secrecy to prevent the plan from being blocked through the abuse of power being wielded by Humanity's patriarchal human egos at the time. Jesus and Mary Magdalene were equal partners, and together they God Victoriously accomplished the Immaculate Concept of their Divine Missions.

During what is referred to as *"the lost 18 years,"* Jesus and Mary Magdalene studied in the mystery schools of India, Tibet, and Egypt. When it was time to begin their mission of anchoring the archetypes for the return of our Mother God and Humanity's return to Christ Consciousness, Jesus demonstrated for all the world to see the imperative first step— the return of the Divine Feminine, our Mother God, the Holy Spirit.

Our Immortal Victorious Threefold Flames represent the true meaning of the Holy Trinity: the blue Flame of our Father God's Power, the pink Flame of our Mother God's Love—the Holy Spirit, and the gold Flame of the Son or Daughter of God's Wisdom—the Christ. When we closed our Heart Chakra and forced our Mother God to withdraw, we lost awareness of the Divine Feminine and the true understanding of the Holy Spirit. We knew this aspect of Divinity was the Holy Comforter and the Love Nature of God, but we no longer knew that the Holy Spirit is our Mother God. Instead, we thought of the Holy Spirit as a masculine aspect of our Father God.

Only when the masculine and feminine polarities of our Father-Mother God are balanced within us, and our Crown Chakras are fully open can we reconnect with our Christ Selves and attain Christ Consciousness. In order to help Humanity accomplish this, the anchoring of the archetype for the return of our Mother God was the first step of Jesus and Mary Magdalene's Divine Mission.

At the age of 30, Jesus and Mary Magdalene came to the banks of the Jordan River, where Jesus immersed himself in the sacred water element. Water represents the emotional strata for the Earth as well as the emotional bodies for Humanity. Once Jesus was in the water, he participated in a Divine Ceremony through which he served as a surrogate on behalf of all Humanity. In that ceremony, John the Baptist washed away the sins of the world by Baptizing Jesus with the Love of our Mother God—the Holy Spirit. Through that Baptism of the Holy Spirit, Jesus and Mary Magdalene anchored the archetype for the return of our Mother God.

We have all seen pictures of Jesus standing in the Jordan River with the Dove of the Holy Spirit descending into his Crown Chakra. In that moment, Jesus' right-brain hemisphere was brought into perfect balance with his left-brain hemisphere. His spiritual brain centers were activated, and his Crown Chakra was opened to full breadth. When this occurred, Jesus became the Christ grown to full stature, and his mission of modeling Humanity's Divine Potential as a Beloved Child of God began in earnest. Simultaneously, Mary Magdalene experienced the same anointing through a Baptism of the Holy Spirit. At that moment, Jesus and Mary Magdalene became the Avatars of the Piscean Age.

For the next three years, Jesus modeled to the world the path of Oneness and Divine Love that each of us must follow in order to reconnect with our Christ Selves and to reclaim our Divine Birthright as Sons and Daughters of God. Day in and day out, Mary Magdalene supported Jesus with her love, and held the sacred space for the fulfillment of the Immaculate Concept of both his and her facets of their Divine Missions.

The path of Oneness and Divine Love is the only way the Children of God will return to the Heart of our Divine Father and Mother. Jesus demonstrated this path and our Divine Potential through various activities of Light and the miracles he performed. Both he and Mary Magdalene clearly revealed the Oneness of Life through their dedication to each other and their reverence for ALL Life.

Due to the manipulation of our human egos, much of Jesus' mission has been misunderstood. He did not come to establish a new religion. He came to remind every man, woman, and child that we are Divine Children of God. His mission was to demonstrate this Truth by the way he lived his life and to inspire us to do the same. Many believe that Jesus alone is the Divine Child of God, the only begotten Son. They believe that he came to save us and that he did everything for us because we are such lost and depraved souls. Some people have the misconception that if we just speak the words that affirm that we accept Jesus as our personal savior he will save us, without our having to be accountable for how we have used our precious gift of Life. This distorted belief is based in Humanity's deeply ingrained feeling of unworthiness, but it is certainly not what Beloved Jesus taught us.

Jesus' message was that the Divinity within each of us—the Christ—is the true Child of God, the only begotten Son or Daughter. He said throughout his ministry, *"These things I do you shall do, and even greater things than these shall you do."*

There are some other statements in the Bible that also reflect this Truth:

And Jesus answered them, *"Is it not written in your law, I said, 'YE ARE GODS'?"*

*"YE ARE GODS, and all of you are Children of the Most High."*

And from Romans 8: 14-17, *"For as many as are led by the Spirit of God, they are the Sons of God—the Spirit itself beareth witness with our Spirit that we are the Children of God; and if Children, then heirs, heirs of God, JOINT HEIRS WITH CHRIST."*

At the age of 33, Jesus accomplished the final facets of his Divine Mission. Thirty-three is the master number that reflects the Christ made manifest. There is a lot of discussion at this time as to whether Jesus was actually crucified and whether or not he resurrected his body. The Company of Heaven has confirmed that both of these events were vitally important to the fulfillment of Jesus and Mary Magdalene's Divine Plan.

Contrary to the guilt-inducing things we are often told, the reason Jesus was tortured and crucified was not to atone for Humanity's sins, because we are so evil we cannot do it for ourselves. This concept comes from the belief that we are so lowly someone outside of ourselves must save us. This belief perpetuates the notion that we are incapable of saving ourselves, but that is not true. In fact, our Father-Mother God gave each of us the gift of free will and NO ONE is allowed to do this for us. We are each responsible for how we have used our gift of Life.

We lost the awareness of our own Divinity through our free will choices and the misuse of our creative faculties of thought and feeling. Consequently, the only way we will return to Christ Consciousness is through our own endeavors. We must follow the path of Oneness and Divine Love that Jesus modeled for us.

Jesus agreed to be crucified in order to prove to the world that there is *nothing* the fallen human ego can do that will destroy the Divinity within us. His crucifixion and resurrection proved that even if one's physical body is abused, tortured, and crucified, the Christ within is eternal and lives on in our Light Body.

Even though Jesus did not save us in the way many are saying, he did forgive the sins of the world in a very different way. When Jesus was hanging on the cross a Centurion pierced his side with a sword. His intent was to accelerate Jesus' death, and to put him out of his misery. As Jesus' blood and Lifeforce flowed onto the Earth Jesus said, *"Forgive them Father, for they know not what they do."* In that instant, our Father-Mother God allowed the Law of Forgiveness to be initiated as the order of the New Day on Planet Earth.

Prior to that moment, the Children of God were subject solely to the Law of Karma, or the Law of Cause and Effect. After the Law of Forgiveness was established on Earth, we had another option. Humanity could ask for forgiveness for the misuse of our precious gift of Life and be forgiven. We are still subject to the Law of Cause and Effect, but now when we recognize the error of our ways we can ask for forgiveness. Forgiveness transmutes our misqualified energy back into Light before it returns to us as a difficult challenge through the Law of the Circle.

It is important for us to understand that we are not forgiven just because Jesus was here, as some believe. We are forgiven if we recognize our mistakes, ask for forgiveness, and change our behavior patterns.

After Jesus' crucifixion and his resurrection into his Light Body, he had one more very important Truth to reveal to Humanity. It was obvious that the Children of God had been beaten down into a consciousness of unworthiness. Ever since our Ascended brothers and sisters were visible to our sight aeons ago, we had been waiting for someone to come and save us. Jesus realized that because of this low opinion of ourselves, the chances were great that we would misunderstand his mission also.

He and Mary Magdalene came to anchor the archetypes for the return of our Mother God, and to demonstrate for us the path of Oneness and Divine Love that each of us must follow if we are to reconnect with our Christ Selves and return to Christ Consciousness. Jesus knew that our lack of trust in ourselves was overwhelming. The potential was great that we would misconstrue his mission by believing that he had saved us, and that he had done for us the very things he came to demonstrate that we must do for ourselves.

The final facet of Beloved Jesus' mission was to clearly reveal to Humanity that he cannot do this for us, and that we are not saved simply because he was here. Jesus left an example to prove that no matter how dedicated we are to him and his teachings, we are each responsible for our return to Christ Consciousness. In order to accomplish this facet of the Divine Plan, Jesus invoked the assistance of his Beloved Disciples.

After Jesus' resurrection, he remained on Earth for 40 days. During that time, he demonstrated to the Disciples what it was like to experience Christ Consciousness. Jesus expanded his Light Body to envelop the Disciples. Within that radiant Light, the Disciples were lifted up in consciousness so that they could experience what it was like to reconnect with their Christ Selves. In this elevated state, the Disciples remembered their Divine Heritage as Beloved Children of God.

Once they were reconnected with their Christ Selves, the Disciples were able to perform all of the miracles Jesus performed. They quickly learned the lessons that would enable them to continue the mission that had been started by their beloved brother, Jesus. They prepared to spread the Truth of Humanity's Divinity and to teach the path of Oneness and Divine Love that would lead to Christ Consciousness for every evolving soul.

At the end of the 40 days, it was time for Jesus to Ascend into the next phase of his mission. When the Heavens opened and

Jesus Ascended into the Realms of Illumined Truth, it was no longer possible for him to sustain the Disciples in the elevated frequency of Christ Consciousness by enveloping them in his Light Body. Since the Disciples had not attained Christ Consciousness through their own endeavors, once Jesus withdrew his Light Body they began to falter and became afraid.

The Disciples realized that in spite of their great love for Jesus and their dedication to him and his mission, he could not save them or sustain them in Christ Consciousness. It was not enough for them to love him, or for them to accept him as their personal savior. Reaching Christ Consciousness was something each of them would have to accomplish on his own. The most Jesus and Mary Magdalene could do was anchor the archetypes for the return of our Mother God, and demonstrate the path of Oneness and Divine Love that we must each follow in order to return to Christ Consciousness.

For ten days the Disciples struggled with their predicament. On the 50th day after Jesus' resurrection, the day we now call Pentecost, the Disciples realized what they must do in order to attain and sustain Christ Consciousness. On that day, the Disciples entered what was called the *Upper Room.* This was a higher state of consciousness that they each attained by consecrating their lives to the path of Oneness and Divine Love. In that elevated state of consciousness, each of the Disciples opened his heart and from the depths of his Being invoked the return of our Mother God through a Baptism of the Holy Spirit. This time, the Baptism was by Sacred Fire instead of water.

In that instant, the Disciples' right-brain hemispheres were brought into perfect balance with their left-brain hemispheres. Their spiritual brain centers were activated, and their Crown Chakras were opened to full breadth. This allowed the Disciples to reconnect with their Christ Selves. We have all seen depictions of the Disciples after their Baptism by the Holy Spirit on Pentecost. They are shown with a Flame pulsating from their Crown Chakras indicating that they had regained Christ Consciousness, and that their mission of spreading Jesus' teachings to the world was at hand.

On that holy day of Pentecost, the Disciples were given what has been called *the gift of tongues.* This is another aspect of the Piscean Age that has often been misunderstood. The gift of tongues did not mean that the Holy Spirit would speak through the Disciples in unintelligible syllables and sounds for someone to try to decipher. The gift of tongues meant that the Disciples had ability to travel the face of the Earth and to teach the Truth of Humanity's Divinity and the path of Oneness and Divine Love in the language of the people to whom they were speaking. This eliminated the problem of language barriers and ensured the clarity of Jesus' message.

Even with all of the groundwork that was carefully laid during the Piscean Age, Jesus and Mary Magdalene knew that it would be millennia before Humanity would really understand their message and reclaim our Divine Birthright as Beloved Children of God. It was obvious that our human egos were not going to relinquish their patriarchal control easily. The resistance would be great, and every possible effort would be made to suppress the role of Mary Magdalene and the Truth of our Mother God. Jesus confirmed this knowing in Revelations when he stated, *"In the Day of the Seventh Angel, when he shall begin to sound, the mystery of God will be fulfilled and time will be no more."* He said this would involve the Second Coming of the Christ.

The predominant influence flooding the planet during the 2,000 years of the Piscean Age was the Sixth Solar Aspect of Deity. That Aspect of our Father-Mother God reflects the Divine Qualities of Peace, Healing, Devotional Worship, Ministering Grace, the Christ working through the personality, and the Divine Image embodied in flesh. These influences were the perfect support that Jesus and Mary Magdalene needed in order to accomplish their Divine Missions.

The Piscean Age was the Day of the Sixth Angel. Jesus is known as the Prince of Peace because of the influences of the Sixth Solar Aspect of Deity. Jesus' symbol is the fish, because he and Mary Magdalene were the Avatars of the Piscean Age, which is represented by the symbol of the fish.

There is a lot of discussion at this time as to whether Jesus and Mary Magdalene were married and whether or not they had children. In that day, it was part of Jewish Law for men to marry and have children. Jesus and Mary Magdalene were very much a part of the Jewish tradition. The Company of Heaven has verified that they were indeed married, and that they did have a child. Many of the people who believe this think it is proof that Jesus was not crucified, but that is inaccurate. People were married when they were very young in those days. Jesus and Mary Magdalene were married during the lost 18 years. When they came to the Jordan River at the age of 30, they already had their family.

The Beings of Light said that this knowledge is causing some confusion. There is a massive search going on to trace Jesus and Mary Magdalene's bloodline. The Company of Heaven said that this is both inappropriate and a distraction from our Divine Plans. We are all One, and each and every one of us has an important role to play in the unfolding Divine Plan. Who our ancestors were is irrelevant. We will not be allowed to discover the Truth about Jesus and Mary Magdalene's bloodline. If we ever found out who their descendants are, we would make them celebrities, which would be a distraction from their Divine Missions, and it would only cause further separation.

After Jesus' crucifixion, resurrection, and Ascension, plans were set into motion to protect Mary Magdalene from the wrath of the people who wanted to block the awareness of our Mother God. The Essene Brotherhood and Sisterhood, along with Mother Mary, Joseph of Arimathea, John the Beloved, and some of the other disciples, guarded Mary Magdalene and the daughter she and Jesus had conceived.

Mary Magdalene was over-Lighted by the Company of Heaven. She was safely guided to various locations on the planet where she was able to anchor the matrix for the Divine Balance of our Mother God into the body of Mother Earth. This prepared the way for the Day of the Seventh Angel, which would occur during the dawning of the New Age of Aquarius. That would be the day when our Mother God would at last reclaim her rightful place within the hearts of the Children of Earth. It would be a time when Christ Consciousness would once again be birthed in the hearts and minds of Humanity. This would be the fulfillment of the Second Coming of the Christ that was foretold by Jesus.

The Truth about Mary Magdalene's mission and the fact that she was anchoring the matrix for the return of our Mother God was cloaked in secrecy to conceal the plan from the masses. This was necessary in order to prevent the plan from being blocked through the abuse of power being wielded by Humanity's patriarchal human egos.

Her protectors were well aware of her mission, and after her Ascension, they steadfastly held the Immaculate Concept for the return of our Mother God. These selfless exponents of God's Will formed mystery schools and passed the information on in veiled and mysterious symbols that could not be deciphered by the common man or woman.

The newly formed Christian churches had difficulty blocking the ground swell of information that kept surfacing in mysterious ways about Mary Magdalene and her relationship with Jesus, her Beloved Twin Flame. Various gospels were being circulated, which gave conflicting accounts of what really occurred during the pageantry and the founding of what was being considered the Christian Dispensation. Each gospel was an account of the experience and the beliefs of the person who wrote it. These interpretations were made through each person's consciousness, which was often controlled by their human ego.

In 325 AD, the Roman Emperor Constantine decided that the confusion in the Christian doctrine needed to be stopped and that the various factions needed to be unified into one belief system. He called a meeting of over 300 bishops and organized what has been noted as the first Ecumenical Council. This was the Council of Nicaea.

During that gathering, Constantine denounced Arianism, which was founded by the theologian Arius. These teachings taught that Jesus was a Son of God, and that all of the Children of Earth are Sons and Daughters of God. He reiterated that God is within every person, and that people do not need to depend on Human Beings outside of themselves in order to communicate with God or to receive God's Forgiveness.

This belief system interfered greatly with the power and control of the priesthood and the Church, so Constantine ordered Arius to cease and desist in teaching such heresy. At the end of the gathering, Constantine ordered a vote, and all but three bishops signed the Nicaean Creed forbidding Arianism.

Constantine felt this vote of support gave him the right to proceed with his mission. He gathered the 48 gospels that were being circulated amongst the various factions of the

Church. He went through all of them carefully and selected the gospels that indicated that Jesus was Divine—the *only* begotten Son. In all of the 48 gospels, there were only four that indicated that Jesus alone was a Son of God, and that every other Child of God is less than Jesus in God's eyes. These four gospels were unnamed, as were many of the 48 gospels. Constantine made the arbitrary decision to name the gospels he chose to be included in the Bible: Matthew, Mark, Luke and John.

Constantine then proceeded to go through the rest of the teachings to decide what he wanted to include in the Bible. In order to maintain the supreme power of the Church and the patriarchal priesthood, he removed any reference to the relationship between Mary Magdalene and Jesus. He also removed any reference he could identify regarding reincarnation. Constantine's actions redefined the status of Christianity, and formed the basis for the Bible used today throughout the Christian world.

Even with this obvious betrayal of the Truth, the mission of Jesus and Mary Magdalene could not be suppressed. To the total consternation of the Church, the reality of their spiritual and intimate relationship kept surfacing. One by one the seekers of Truth were guided to the mystery schools and secret societies. Little by little they learned about the sacred mission of Jesus and Mary Magdalene.

In 590 AD, Pope Gregory decided that enough was enough. He was determined to once and for all put an end to this threat to the patriarchal supremacy of the Church. With the stroke of his pen, Pope Gregory declared that Mary Magdalene was a prostitute and asserted that she was seething with seven evil spirits. This was the very first time that Mary Magdalene was said to be a prostitute. That unconscionable lie was written nearly 600 years after her embodiment. As far as the Church was concerned, this concocted story squelched the rumors about Jesus and Mary Magdalene's marriage.

In order to maintain a semblance of damage control, the Church leaders tried to transfer the attention from Mary Magdalene to another Mary, Jesus' Mother. This was a futile effort in their attempt to block the awareness of our Mother God, because Beloved Mother Mary was also an important factor in the return of the Divine Feminine.

As these two forerunners of the Divine Feminine progressed through those tumultuous times, Mother Mary protected the Truth about Mary Magdalene by holding the *exoteric* focus of the Divine Mother. At the same time, Mary Magdalene continued her mission of preparing the way for the return of our Mother God through *esoteric* circles and her teachings within the sacred mystery schools and secret societies.

For centuries, the Immaculate Concept of Mary Magdalene's Divine Mission with Beloved Jesus was guarded from the outer world by her valiant protectors. With unfailing tenacity these selfless souls prepared for the Day of the Seventh Angel when the return of our Mother God would be brought to fruition.

Throughout history there are bits and pieces of information regarding the souls who were fulfilling the service of protecting the mission of Mary Magdalene and Jesus, but most of them are terribly distorted and contaminated with misinformation from the patriarchal Church. The groups most noteworthy of protecting this mission were the Essenes, the Cathars, and the Knights Templar.

Within the historic documentations of England, Spain,

France and places throughout the Mediterranean, the mystical stories of the Essenes, Cathars, and the Knights Templar can still be found. The most blatant proof of the Church's attempt to suppress the secret knowledge of the Divine Feminine is revealed in the accounts of the horrific persecution and the brutal demise of these dedicated Lightworkers during the Crusades and the Inquisition.

For the past several decades, Lightworkers have been making pilgrimages to the areas where these atrocities took place. The intent of these pilgrimages is to transmute the etheric records of the pain and suffering involved in protecting the Truth about the return of our Mother God.

## THE WORLD RELIGIONS

Our Father-Mother God never intended for the sacred knowledge that was given to Humanity during the windows of the dawning New Ages to be crystallized into divisive religions. The purpose of this information was to help us reverse the adverse effects of our fall from Grace and awaken us to the Truth of who we are and why we are here. As the sacred knowledge filtered into Humanity's conscious minds Age after Age, the hope was that we would reclaim our Divine Birthright as Beloved Children of God, and learn to become the cocreators we are destined to be. Unfortunately, our human egos missed the point.

Instead of accepting the teachings of the fundamental principles of Oneness and Reverence for ALL Life, which were the initial tenets of *every* world religion, we allowed our human egos to distort the Truth. Without the balance of our Mother God's Love, our egos manipulated the information flowing to Earth in ways that would allow the abuse of our masculine power to reign supreme. Our fear-based, fragmented egos were desperately afraid of losing control of our Earthly bodies. They were functioning from the belief that in order to survive they must lie, cheat, steal, and kill. They believed that was the only way they could maintain control and power.

I want to state clearly that the basis of the teachings of all of the world religions began with positive intent. These original doctrines were based in Truth and given to Humanity by the Beings of Light with the Divine Purpose of moving us forward in the Light. It is only when our human egos got involved, and the original tenets were changed to became manipulative, fear-based, and controlling that things went awry.

All we have to do to confirm the resistance our human egos initiated in order to maintain the power they usurped from our Christ Selves, is observe what has taken place in the various world religions over the Ages. Our egos' distortion of the Truth was done with the intent of manipulating Humanity through separation and fear. These distortions were taught to us as facts by the world religions. This intentional misinformation has caused the divisiveness and the incredible pain and suffering that has been perpetuated through the world religions over the past 12,000 years.

It is interesting to note that the *only* way our Christ Selves can regain control of our Earthly bodies is for us to open our Heart Chakras, and for us to allow the return of our Mother God's Love—the Holy Spirit. Balancing the Divine Feminine within our hearts and brains is the key to Humanity's return to Christ Consciousness. This is true regardless of what religion we belong to. Yet, almost every world religion emphatically denies the existence of our Mother God. They have even gone so far as to prevent women from being involved in the hierarchy of the religion. The vast majority of world religions are controlled by men to the extent that the participation of women in the hierarchy is actually forbidden. This is an obvious demonstration of our egos' attempt to suppress the Divine Feminine within each of us, in order to maintain control of our Earthly bodies and our lives through the abuse of masculine power.

Any world religion, from any time frame, that has condoned the abuse of our masculine power is not following Divine Guidance based in Truth. Any religion that has condoned the killing of people or supported the lack of reverence for Life in any form is being manipulated by our human egos. Any religion that is suppressing the knowledge of our Mother God's Love and the Divine Feminine is leading people astray.

The teachings in the scriptures of the various world religions that talk about "holy wars" are also being manipulated by our human egos. These teachings are not referring to killing people who disagree with our perception of the Truth. They are talking about Humanity's inner struggle—the battle between our human egos and our Christ Selves. Even the intent of this "holy war" is not to kill our human egos. It is for us to love that aspect of our personality into the Light, so our Christ Selves can once again take command of our Earthly bodies.

During the first 1,500 years of the Piscean Age, the terrible conflict between the man-made interpretations of the various world religions raged on. Many people were afraid to accept the new information that was brought to the world by Jesus and Mary Magdalene, because it conflicted with what they were being taught in their religions. Many others had developed distorted perceptions of the new information, and tried to force their beliefs on people through violence and the threat of death.

A little over 500 years ago, in the midst of that herculean struggle, something happened that would change the course of history for the Planet Earth and all her Life. At that time, the Earth was considered the dark star in the system of Alpha and Omega.

Humanity was enmeshed in what is historically called the Dark Ages. The Company of Heaven was striving to help our Christ Selves burst the bonds of our human egos, but our progress was painfully slow. It seemed as though it would take aeons of time for our Christ Selves to reclaim dominion of our Earthly bodies. Our human egos were doing everything possible to keep us from remembering that we are Children of God on Earth for the purpose of learning how to become cocreators with our Father-Mother God.

Then without warning, in a moment that caught even the Beings of Light serving the Earth by surprise, our Father-Mother God alerted the Universe that the time had arrived for another Shift of the Ages. This meant that the Solar System of Alpha and Omega would be Inbreathed into the timeless, spaceless frequencies of the 5th Dimension. Since the Earth had taken on the fallen souls from the other 143 planets in this Solar System during the last Shift of the Ages, those planets were all ready to make this evolutionary ascent up the Spiral of Evolution. The Earth, however, was in a very different situation.

We were still floundering in the densest frequencies of the 3rd Dimension. It had been millions of years since the last Shift of the Ages, and after all that time we had not been able to catch up with our sisters and brothers in the 4th Dimension. The chance of our Ascending into the 5th-Dimensional frequencies of God's Infinite Perfection without being vaporized was nonexistent.

Everyone in the Universe realized the dire predicament the Earth was in, and they knew we got into this mess out of the greatest act of Divine Love the Children of God had ever expressed for their sisters and brothers. In one great unified effort, the entire Company of Heaven made a heartfelt plea to our Father-Mother God asking for Divine Intervention on our behalf.

The Beings of Light said never before had the entire Universe joined together to assist one small planet. It was an unprecedented outpouring of Divine Love. Our Father-Mother God evaluated the situation, and agreed to grant the Earth a Cosmic Dispensation. That dispensation gave Humanity and this planet a 500-year period of Grace. During that time we had to catch up with the rest of our Solar System so we could Ascend into the 5th Dimension. If we could not accomplish that mighty feat, we would have to be left behind.

# CHAPTER SEVEN

# A 500-YEAR PERIOD OF DIVINE GRACE

Five hundred years seems like a very long time, but in the timeless, spaceless frequencies of the Universe, it is an instant. In order to prevent this Cosmic Dispensation from interfering with the Divine Timing of the Shift of the Ages, our Father-Mother God enveloped the Earth and all her Life in the frequencies of the Eternal Moment of Now. Then a clarion call was sent forth by the Beings of Light serving the Earth asking for suggestions and ideas that might help Humanity awaken and catch up with the rest of our Solar System. It was imperative that these plans not interfere with our free will.

We had not been able to move into the 4th Dimension in millions of years, so for us to accomplish this in just 500 years would be a monumental feat in itself, but we were being asked to do much more than that. We had to not only Ascend into the 4th Dimension, we had to be ready to Ascend into the 5th Dimension during the Shift of the Ages. Never in the whole of Creation had a planet gone through two dimensional shifts in such a short period of time, especially a planet that had fallen into such dense frequencies of vibration. Usually it takes millions of years for a planet and the Life evolving upon that planet to evolve enough to Ascend from one dimension into a higher dimension. Without question, the Earth was embarking on an experiment that had never been attempted in any system of worlds.

Innumerable plans were presented to Alpha and Omega and the Beings of Light serving the Earth. The plans that were chosen were believed to have the greatest potential for raising our vibrations and our consciousness in time for the shift. These plans were projected simultaneously into the mental stratum of Earth and began to filter into the consciousness of Humanity. The main focus involved the greatest need of the hour for Humanity, which was the return of our Mother God and the path of Divine Love and Reverence for Life that Humanity must to learn to live by.

When the Children of Earth closed our Heart Chakras and blocked the portal that allowed our Mother God's Love to flow into our bodies, we also created a block in the portal for our Mother God's Love that sustains the body of Mother Earth. This blocked portal allowed only a minuscule fraction of our Mother God's Love to flow into the planet. This prevented the Elemental Kingdom from maintaining Humanity's Earthly bodies and the body of Mother Earth in a state of vibrant health. In order for us to raise our vibrations enough to be able to withstand the 4th and 5th Dimensions, this situation had to be corrected. So one of the plans to be implemented at the beginning of our 500 year period of Grace, was the opening for the portal of our Mother God's Love in the body of Mother Earth.

The Earth is a living breathing organism, and she too has the masculine and feminine polarities of our Father-Mother God flowing through her body. The masculine polarity of our Father God enters the Earth as a tremendous shaft of Light in the area of the Himalayan Mountains near Tibet. That is why this is such a powerful focus of spirituality, and why there has been such an abuse of masculine power there since our fall from Grace. The feminine polarity of our Mother God enters the Earth in an area of Bolivia, in South America. This location is near Lake Titicaca, in the Andes Mountains. Since Humanity closed our Heart Chakras aeons ago, this portal of our Mother God has been almost dormant.

The Company of Heaven was not allowed to just open this portal for us. Humanity had inadvertently created this situation through our free-will choices, so we had to be instrumental in reopening the portal. In order to succeed, we needed to focus the power of our thoughts and feelings on our Mother God's Love. Since we were oblivious to our Mother God's existence, a plan was set into motion to draw the attention of the people in the area of the feminine portal to the closest expression of the Divine Mother that they were capable of understanding. This was the Presence of Mother Mary.

Between December 8 and 12, 1531, Mother Mary appeared to a peasant named Juan Diego. These apparitions took place on the hill of Tepeyac, near Mexico City. This aspect of Mother Mary became known as Our Lady of Guadalupe. The news of the apparitions and the story of the miracle of the image of roses she left on the cloak of Juan Diego, spread throughout Mexico and South America like wild fire. A powerful resurgence of devotion to Mother Mary—the Divine Mother— ensued, which is prevalent to this very day. This adoration to the Divine Mother opened the portal for the feminine polarity of our Mother God once again. As the Love of our Mother God flowed into the body of Mother Earth, Humanity's Heart Flames quickened and our right-brain hemispheres began to slowly awaken.

The next phase of the plan was designed to accelerate the awakening of Humanity's creative right-brain hemispheres, which had been almost dormant since the fall. In the middle of the 14th century we were living in the Dark Ages and our affinity for culture and the arts was practically nonexistent. In order to stimulate our creative right brains, the Company of Heaven projected the wisdom of the arts into the mental strata of Earth. As this sacred knowledge filtered into Humanity's conscious minds, the Renaissance began to flourish in Florence, Italy.

The expansion of art, music, dance, literature, and every other creative facet of the Renaissance moved Humanity into a level of civility that we had not experienced for a very long time. The movement in Italy spread throughout Europe, signaling the end of the Dark Ages and the beginning of modern history. The

Renaissance inspired civil liberty and a new internal order of culture and political development. It was the beginning of Humanity's awakening and a crucial stage in the process of liberating the human mind from our ego's paralyzing grip of fear and misinformation. In the midst of unrivaled, barbaric darkness, the Renaissance birthed a civilization of a higher order.

As our right-brain hemispheres were stimulated with new levels of creativity, more of the Love of our Mother God was able to flow into our lives. Much of the art painted by the great masters focused on some of the main players in the Piscean Age. Joseph, Mother Mary, and Jesus, who symbolically represented the Holy Trinity, were depicted in many of the Renaissance paintings. This focus of Humanity's attention on the Holy Trinity helped to expand the Immortal Victorious Threefold Flame in our hearts.

Another plan that was set into motion a little over 500 years ago involved the attempt to unify the family of Humanity. During the Dark Ages our human egos manipulated us through fear and separation. Any difference in race, nationality, religion, gender, culture, social, or economic status increased our fear and amplified our lack of trust in each other. The Company of Heaven decided that one of the most important things Humanity needed to remember is that we are all One. To fulfill this need, a plan to anchor the archetype for Humanity's return to Oneness was projected into the mental strata of Earth.

It was clear to the Company of Heaven that we required an outer-world example of the family of Humanity living together in harmony. This would be a model, the microcosm of the macrocosm, involving people from all over the world respecting and honoring each other; an example of people reveling in each others' diversities, as they shared their unique gifts and talents for the highest good of all concerned. This would be a demonstration of

Humanity living together in equality, freedom, prosperity, and the unified pursuit of happiness.

As this facet of the plan filtered into Humanity's consciousness, the man known as Christopher Columbus received the Divine Guidance to begin searching for a New World where the archetype for Humanity's return to Oneness could be anchored. The description he gave of his mission to Queen Isabella of Spain and those who would be funding the project, was that he would be seeking new trade routes, but the underlying intent of Christopher Columbus' flotilla was a much higher goal.

I know there is a lot of negativity projected onto Christopher Columbus, because he is blamed for the atrocities inflicted on the indigenous peoples of the Americas by his crew and the Europeans who followed him to America. The Beings of Light have revealed important information about this situation to help all of us understand the bigger picture.

When Christopher Columbus received the Divine Inspiration to cross the seas in search of the New World, no one believed he would survive such a journey. He was forced to take with him as his crew, prison inmates and demented souls from mental institutions. When those troubled and violent souls arrived in the New World, they were not restrained by any laws. This allowed their human egos to revert to their basest instincts and destructive behavior patterns, without constraints. In spite of that tragic situation, Christopher Columbus was able to successfully anchor the archetypes of Humanity's Oneness in the New World.

One of the things the Beings of Light want us to realize is that 500 years ago, Humanity's human egos were running amuck in every location on the planet. Sometimes it is reported as though the indigenous peoples of the Americas were all peace-loving people who were living together in harmony and love. Then, all of a sudden, these vicious Europeans came and killed them all. In Truth, there were very violent tribal wars going on in the Americas long before the Europeans came. There were human sacrifices and brutal wars over territories and sacred lands. This certainly does not in any way justify what the Europeans did, but we need to put into perspective how out of control Humanity's egos were. We were all afraid of each other, and we violently protected what we thought we needed for survival. That is exactly what Christopher Columbus' facet of the plan was hoping to correct.

Christopher Columbus was one of the embodiments of the Ascended Master St. Germain. St. Germain is known in the Realms of Illumined Truth as a Son of Freedom. He is an exponent of the Violet Flame of God's Infinite Perfection, and he will be a predominant influence in helping Humanity return to Christ Consciousness during the Age of Aquarius.

In his mission as Christopher Columbus, St. Germain was responsible for reopening the largest portal for the Violet Flame on the planet. This portal became dormant when our Mother God was forced to withdraw her Love after the fall. This portal covers an area including the Dominican Republic, the Caribbean Islands, Cuba, Florida, and the surrounding seas. It was not by chance that the flotilla of Christopher Columbus was first drawn to Santo Domingo. When he arrived in that location, the Company of Heaven joined with Christopher Columbus as he served as a surrogate on behalf of all Humanity. Through the unified efforts of Heaven and Earth, the portal of the Violet Flame of God's Infinite Perfection was opened to full breadth.

When the Violet Flame flowed through the portal into the physical plane of Earth, the land mass now known as the United States of America was flooded with the balanced frequencies of our Father God's Power and our Mother God's Love. This was a necessary first step in anchoring the archetypes of Humanity's Oneness. Then, through a process of Divine Ceremonies that were orchestrated by Christopher Columbus and the Company of Heaven, the archetypes for Humanity's Oneness were successfully anchored in the New World.

The word AMERICA is an anagram for the I AM RACE. This name plus the frequencies of the archetypes for Humanity's Oneness, created a forcefield of Divine Love that drew the family of Humanity from all over the planet to the New World. The term "*I AM Race*" represents a race of God-Conscious souls comprised of ALL races, religions, cultures, creeds, nationalities, and every social and economic status. The I AM Race was to be the microcosm of the family of Humanity living together in harmony, equality, prosperity, happiness, and every other glorious thing that we experienced prior to our fall from Grace.

Our human egos were in charge at that time, so the Company of Heaven knew we were not going to instantaneously become fearless, loving people. Just as Jesus knew it would take millennia for us to understand his message of returning to Christ Consciousness, it was clear that it would take a period of time for Humanity to grasp the concept that we are all One. In an attempt to inspire our egos to relinquish the power they had usurped from our Christ Selves, a plan was initiated to help us see what would occur if we did not reclaim the path of Divine Love and Oneness.

In this plan, the Company of Heaven wanted Humanity to see what would occur if we allowed our human egos to continue to manipulate our lives. To accomplish this goal, a man in France was chosen to receive the Divinely Inspired visions that would reveal to Humanity what would occur if we continued the course we were on. About 500 years ago, Michel de Nostredame, known to us as Nostradamas, began transcribing his famous Quatrains. Many people have criticized these visions as being too negative, but the intent of the prophecies was to show us where we were headed if we did not reclaim our Mother God's Love. Interestingly, the name "Nostradamas" means "Our Lady."

Nostradamas stated that his predicted events were an indication of the pain and suffering Humanity would create for ourselves if we did not change our course of direction. The Divine Intent of this information was not to perpetuate fear, it was to motivate us into positive action.

Any Divinely Inspired prophecy that foretells of an upcoming negative event is intended to avert that event. *A fulfilled negative prophecy is a failed prophecy.* The Company of Heaven never gives information about negative events if Humanity cannot change what is predicted to happen. The only time the Beings of Light reveal negative things to us is if we can do something to correct the situation. If there is a challenging event that Humanity needs to experience, and we cannot do anything to change it, the Beings of Light will not tell us about it. That would only amplify our fear, which would be a distraction from our Divine Plans.

When people are predicting negative events and indicating that there is nothing we can do to stop them, the information is *not* coming from the Realms of Illumined Truth. It is misinformation coming from either our human egos or the psychic-astral plane, with the intent of keeping us immobilized through fear.

In spite of the various plans that were set into motion 500 years ago, our human egos were not willing to release their control. Many people responded to their hearts' call and came to the New

World, but most of them brought all of their fears and obsolete behavior patterns with them. People felt that the battle to free themselves from British rule was justified in an effort to gain independence, but our human egos did not stop there. We inflicted unconscionable pain and suffering on our sisters and brothers through slavery, prejudice, greed, the abuse of power, and fanatical religious beliefs.

Fortunately, when the Founding Fathers for the United States of America came to this country they had an inner knowing about their Divine Missions. When they set foot on the land, their Christ Selves enveloped them in the Divine Balance of the Violet Flame. This allowed the Company of Heaven to effectively work with these dedicated men.

With the over-Lighting guidance of the Beings of Light, our Founding Fathers transcribed onto paper the archetypes for the Oneness of Humanity. These words of Truth formed the template for the New World. The sacred documents for the United States of America clearly state the principles of Oneness and equality that are necessary in order for the family of Humanity to live in peace. Unfortunately, our human egos have done everything they possibly can to block the manifestation of these Truths.

After all of these facets of the Divine Plan were in place, the Company of Heaven reevaluated the situation. It was clear that a few people on the planet were awakening and some progress was being made by those souls, but there were millions who were still being controlled and manipulated by their human egos. The Beings of Light felt the potential was great that the masses of Humanity would not awaken in time to make the shift into the 4th Dimension, let alone be ready to Ascend into the 5th Dimension. It was obvious that the Earth would need superhuman assistance if we were going to succeed in this experiment.

# DIVINE INTERVENTION

With permission from our Father-Mother God, Alpha and Omega sent forth a clarion call asking for volunteers who would be willing to embody on Earth to help free this planet from the snare of Humanity's human egos. In response, literally billions of highly evolved souls from dimensions beyond anything the Earth had ever experienced volunteered to come to Earth to help in this holy endeavor. These souls would be subject to the laws affecting the Earth, so they would have to receive the Band of Forgetfulness like all incoming souls. Since the Ascended Masters became such a distraction for Humanity during the time we call Greek Mythology, our Father-Mother God decreed that these highly evolved volunteers would not be distinguishable from the Children of Earth in any way.

The hope was that since these souls were not involved with the fall or the creation of the maladies existing on Earth, they would have a better chance of awakening quickly. This would enable them to create an upward flow of consciousness that would lift Humanity's focus of attention, thus helping us to awaken and to reconnect with the Realms of Illumined Truth.

Most of these advanced souls had never experienced anything like the negativity existing on this planet, so there was concern that they might get caught up in the chaos like the Children of Earth did with the coming of the fallen souls. To test the waters for this experiment, our Father-Mother God decided to allow just a few of these selfless Sons and Daughters of God to embody on Earth at a time.

For the first 400 years of our 500-year period of Grace, these highly evolved souls came to Earth one by one. They did what they could to add to the Light of the world and to help shift

Humanity's consciousness. Some of them may be the adepts that we have heard or read about, but in most instances these powerful Beings of Light served Humanity and fulfilled their missions without the awareness of the outer world.

Toward the end of the 1800s, the Earth was moving out of the frequencies of Pisces, but we had not moved into the full embrace of Aquarius. We were entering the window of opportunity that is referred to as *"the dawn of the New Age."* In alignment with what normally occurs during the dawn of a New Age, our Father-Mother God and Alpha and Omega evaluated the progress being made on Earth. The plans that were initiated at the beginning of our 500-year period of Grace were succeeding to a degree, but there were still colossal amounts of negative energy from Humanity's accumulated miscreations that had to be transmuted back into Light.

These destructive energies involved lifetimes of hatred and violence that had been perpetuated by our human egos. Since we are all One, every particle of Life is interrelated, interconnected, and interdependent. There is no separation. What affects one facet of Life affects all Life. What this means in very practical terms is that this accumulation of Humanity's negative thoughts, feelings, words, and actions had to be brought to the surface and transmuted back into Light if *any* of us were going to be ready to make the shift in time.

Energy cannot be destroyed. It can only be transformed. We cannot just say "cancel, cancel" and clear lifetimes worth of our egos' abuse of power. We had to become aware of our past transgressions of the Laws of Divine Love and Reverence for Life, so that we could invoke the Light of God and transmute these gross mutations back into their original perfection.

We created every abominable human miscreation by misusing the precious atomic and subatomic particles and waves of energy our Father-Mother God had given to us as our Lifeforce. Through our free-will choices, we accepted our gift of Life and then distorted that harmonious energy into all manner of pain and suffering. Now, in order for us to move forward with the rest of our Solar System, there was no other option than for us to experience the results of our miscreations, so we could transmute them back into Light.

Knowing the urgency of the hour, our Father-Mother God issued a Cosmic Edict that gave the highly evolved souls permission to intervene in the purging and healing of Humanity's miscreations in unprecedented ways. For the first time ever, these selfless Sons and Daughters of God were given permission to join with the Children of Earth and to actually take on some of the mass consciousness and the collective karmic liabilities Humanity had been miscreating for millions of years. This meant that these evolved souls would have to embody in areas where the maladies of Earth and the densest frequencies of pain and suffering were being played out in the lives of Humanity.

When our Father-Mother God and Alpha and Omega made their evaluation, they saw that during the past 400 years the experiment involving the advanced souls had made a real difference. Even though only a few of those souls were allowed to come to Earth at a time, they were adding to the Light of the world in ways that exceeded all expectations. Since there were only 100 years left in our period of Grace, our Father-Mother God decided to expand that facet of the experiment. Our God Parents issued a Fiat directing Alpha and Omega to open the floodgates of Heaven, and to allow these precious volunteers to embody on Earth by the *millions*.

These powerful Beings of Light willingly embodied in every corner of the world. Many of them made the sacrifice of incarnating into the most oppressive frequencies of darkness. These were the locations on the planet where Humanity was experiencing the greatest pain and suffering. They knew that the areas where Humanity's human egos were inflicting atrocities upon each other would have to be exposed in the Light of God and brought to the surface to be healed. These Beings of Light believed that they would be able to transcend the pain more easily than the Children of Earth who had been beaten into the pits of despair for millennia.

When we look historically at the horrific experiences Humanity has gone through during the past 100 years, we get a glimpse of the sacrifice our sisters and brothers made on our behalf. They assisted the Children of Earth and brought our human miscreations to the surface by volunteering to experience devastating wars, religious persecution, plagues, natural disasters, poverty, hunger, hatred, greed, corruption, violence, and the unbridled abuse of power by our human egos. Through their lives and often through their deaths, these precious souls brought to the attention of Humanity the rampant miscreations our human egos were perpetuating on this planet.

Some of these souls awakened fast enough to consciously remember why they were going through such painful experiences, but many of them did not. Nevertheless, they God Victoriously went through the experiences that they volunteered to heal. Their sacrifice purged a great deal of Humanity's collective negativity and catapulted the Children of Earth forward in the Light. As people all over the world witnessed and experienced our inhumane behavior toward each other, we opened our hearts in new and profound ways. The love and compassion we developed when we witnessed the pain and suffering of our sisters and brothers, softened our hearts and allowed more of our Mother God's Love to flow into our lives.

In addition to the souls who volunteered to embody in the densest frequencies of Humanity's pain and suffering, there were those who embodied in areas that would allow them to speed up Humanity's technological advancement. These souls lifted up in consciousness and tapped into the patterns of perfection in the Causal Body of God. Their goal was to improve the conditions of the world through advanced technology. The discoveries and inventions they brought to the world accelerated our progress in ways that cannot be logically explained by our normal evolutionary process.

The quantum leap we made from the 1800s, when we had just discovered the telephone, combustion engine, and electricity, to the advanced technology we have today, does not follow any previously known pace of evolution. It is the tremendous influx of the advanced souls that is responsible for this unprecedented shift of consciousness.

Unfortunately, much of the technology has been hijacked by Humanity's wayward human egos. The knowledge has been corrupted and used for destructive purposes that have caused a great deal of harm. We have abused the technology, and created things like nuclear weapons, designer diseases, and industries that have caused the catastrophic pollution of the Earth and the gross imbalance in the distribution of wealth. Needless to say, this was not part of the plan.

In order to try to curtail this appalling abuse of power, another plan was implemented to help Humanity reconnect with the Realms of Illumined Truth. The Beings of Light were standing in readiness awaiting the opportunity to guide and assist us in our awakening process, but in most instances we were oblivious to their presence. To rectify this situation, our Father-Mother God gave the Company of Heaven permission to reach through the psychic-astral plane to meet us half way. This meant that Humanity would be able to communicate with the Beings of Light and the Realms of Truth much more easily.

When this facet of the plan was initiated, awakening souls all over the world began to tap into the sacred knowledge that had been taught in the esoteric mystery schools for aeons of time. Because of the abuse of power being wielded by the human egos associated with the various world religions, these Truths had been hidden from the masses. The sacred knowledge was taught in secret societies in order to protect it from being corrupted or destroyed.

Once the Beings of Light were given permission to come through the veil to meet us half way, the floodgates of sacred knowledge opened. The information flowed into the mental strata of Earth making these Truths available to the masses of Humanity. The term *"esoteric"* became obsolete, and all information from the Realms of Illumined Truth became *"exoteric."* The mystical teachings of Humanity's origins and the path of Divine Love and Oneness became available to the masses through every conceivable open door. Even many of the world religions began to expand their teachings to include the principles of Divine Love and the acceptance of all peoples in more truthful and inclusive ways.

Many metaphysical organizations began to form, which taught various interpretations of the information pouring forth from the Realms of Truth. People began to learn about the existence of the Violet Flame, and how it could help us to transmute our human miscreations. We began to understand who the Beings of Light in the Realms of Illumined Truth really are, and how they can assist us in our Earthly sojourns. The Company of Heaven gave us powerful tools to help us fulfill our Divine Plans and to increase our ability to add to the Light of the world.

As the advanced souls awakened, the Children of Earth awakened with them. In every corner of the planet people gathered together to invoke the Light of God. Their intent was to help Humanity transmute the painful miscreations our human egos had manifested through the abuse of power.

This shift of consciousness was so pervasive that every single day *billions* of souls on this planet turned their attention toward a higher power and, in one way or another, asked God for Divine Intervention in their lives. No prayer goes unanswered, so this overwhelming heart call from the masses of Humanity allowed our Father-Mother God and the Company of Heaven to intervene in our lives in more powerful ways than we had ever experienced.

Day by day, the Light of God increased on Earth. In every 24-hour period, the Christ Self of every single person on the planet raised their energy, vibration, and consciousness the maximum that Cosmic Law would allow. This moved the Earth and all her Life forward in the Light a quantum leap, which greatly increased our potential of succeeding in the unprecedented experiment we were going through.

To this very day, billions of souls around the world are invoking the Light of God on a daily basis. These precious people are Lightworkers, and they are assisting with the shift of consciousness that is taking place within the hearts and minds of all Humanity. This is true even if they are not yet aware of who they are or the bigger picture of the Divine Plan that is unfolding on Earth.

It is actually immaterial if a person is one of the highly evolved souls from the Realms of Light who have come to help the Children of Earth, or if they are one of the original Children of Earth, or if they are one of the fallen souls who came to Earth and are now awakening and returning to the path of Oneness and Divine Love.

We are all One, and every one of us is embodied on Earth during this auspicious time for the same purpose. We are here because we agreed to help the Earth and ALL her Life Ascend into the 5th Dimension safely.

Every person who invokes the Light of God is a powerful Lightworker, even if he or she does not realize how important the prayers and invocations they are making are for the salvation of Humanity and the Earth. Every prayer, regardless of how small, adds to the Light of the world. Every atomic and subatomic particle and wave of Light we invoke from the Heart of God helps to transmute our human egos' miscreations.

In the short span of 100 years, the influx of highly evolved souls quadrupled the population of Earth. There is a lot of concern that this population explosion is going to result in our demise, but that will not happen. Alpha and Omega would never have allowed this tremendous influx of advanced souls if it was going to cause more harm than good. This is a temporary situation, and when we complete this experiment, these souls will return to their previous locations. The Children of Earth will then continue our learning experiences on this planet until it is time for us to move into the next level of our evolutionary process.

The influx of advanced souls helped to awaken Humanity and shift the consciousness of the masses in ways that transcended even the expectations of Heaven. This did not mean that Humanity's work was finished, but it did mean that the Earth and the souls evolving upon her had raised our vibrations and balanced the Love of our Mother God enough to withstand the shift into the 4th Dimension. This was a monumental accomplishment, and it tangibly proved *"The Light of God is ALWAYS Victorious, and WE are that Light!"*

The next urgent need for Humanity was for us to raise our frequency of vibration fast enough to be able to withstand our Ascension into the 5th Dimension. This had never been done in the short time that was being allotted to us, but we had no other option if we were going to prevent the Earth and all her Life from being left behind. To assist with this facet of the experiment, our sisters and brothers throughout the whole of Creation intensified their efforts to help us. Through the unified efforts of Heaven and Earth, every conceivable assistance was given to Humanity and the Earth to try to accomplish this colossal mission.

# CHAPTER EIGHT

# HARMONIC CONVERGENCE

Harmonic Convergence was an amazing event that took place August 15-17, 1987. After the purging and incredible shift of consciousness that Humanity experienced during the previous 100 years, we were ready for the next step of our awakening process. The influx of Light that occurred during Harmonic Convergence changed the course of history for Humanity. It brought to fruition our 500-year period of Grace, and triggered the initial impulse of Earth's Ascension into the 4th Dimension.

The prophesies of the Hopi, Lakota Sioux, and various other Native American tribes, as well as prophesies from the ancient Mayan civilizations, all foretold of a life-changing event that would take place during the celestial alignments of August 15-17, 1987. Some described the event as *a spiritual initiation into Illumination.* They said this initiation would create a quantum leap in consciousness for all Humanity. The prophesies revealed that this event would tip the scales into a new paradigm of planetary healing and transformation.

That feat was accomplished through the unified efforts of Lightworkers around the world, and the entire Company of Heaven. During those special days in August 1987, Lightworkers responded to their heart's call and traveled to sacred sites and powerful activation points all over the planet. Some people were consciously aware of what was taking place, but many were just intuitively responding to a subtle inner knowing. The sacred sites and power spots Lightworkers were being drawn to were acupuncture points along the meridians of the *crystal grid system* in the body of Mother Earth. This system is the same as the acupuncture points and the meridians associated with the Chakra systems in our physical bodies.

On August 15, 1987, the 4th-Dimensional frequencies of the 12 Solar Aspects of Deity—the Circle of the Sacred Twelve—were projected from the very Heart of our Father-Mother God into the Crown Chakra of Mother Earth. This is the location we refer to as "*Diamond Head*" in the Hawaiian Islands. This area was originally part of the massive continent of Lemuria where the fallen souls from the other 143 planets in our Solar System first embodied on Earth. This is where the Children of Earth's initial fall from Grace took place.

Once the Light from the 4th-Dimensional Circle of the Sacred Twelve entered Mother Earth's Crown Chakra, it descended into the Sun of Even Pressure in the center of the Earth. After being securely anchored in Mother Earth's Heart Flame, the Light expanded out through the crystal grid system. The Light blazed into every acupuncture point along the Earth's meridians.

The Christ Selves of the Lightworkers who were gathered at each acupuncture point inbreathed the 4th-Dimensional Light and anchored it in the Lightworkers' Heart Flames. This process secured the frequencies of the 4th Dimension in the physical plane. Humanity's 3rd-Dimensional planetary Christ Selves were raised in vibration into the frequency of our 4th-Dimensional Solar Christ Presences. Through this miraculous activity of Light, Humanity's Christ Selves and our Solar Christ Presences merged into One magnificent Being of Light.

Once that phase of the plan was successfully accomplished, our Solar Christ Presences inbreathed our 3rd-Dimensional Planetary Spine and our sevenfold Chakra system into the embrace of our 4th-Dimensional Solar Spine and twelvefold Solar Chakra System. Our two spines merged into one 4th-Dimensional Solar Spine with twelve Solar Chakras. This occurred within every man, woman, and child whether we were consciously aware of it or not.

For the next three days, Humanity's Solar Christ Presences integrated these 4th-Dimensional frequencies into our physical, etheric, mental, and emotional bodies at an atomic cellular level. Our human egos fought tooth and nail to stop this influx of Light, but the awakening that had taken place during the previous 100 years gave our Solar Christ Presences enough influence in our lives to block our egos' interference.

After Harmonic Convergence, our egos still had a powerful grip on our Earthly bodies, but now we were existing in both worlds, and our Solar Christ Presences were more involved. We could consciously choose which frequency of vibration we wanted to live in each day. Did we want to abide in the frequencies of our Solar Christ Presence in the 4th Dimension, or in the frequencies of our fragmented, fear-based human ego in the 3rd Dimension? The problem, of course, was that there were millions of people who had not awakened enough to realize that they had this choice.

After our initial Ascent up the Spiral of Evolution into the 4th Dimension, things began to happen at an accelerated pace. Lightworkers all over the world were more conscious of the inner guidance from our Solar Christ Presences and the Company of Heaven. We responded to these inner promptings by increasing the activities of Light we were orchestrating and participating in.

Day by day, the Light of God increased on Earth. This was wonderful, but often confusing. Whenever the Light of God increased on Earth, it seemed to exacerbate many of the painful things that were happening in people's lives. This often made the Lightworkers feel as if their prayers were not being answered or that their efforts were in vain. In response to these inaccurate perceptions, the Company of Heaven has given us greater clarity and encouragement.

## THE INFLUX OF GOD'S LIGHT

An accelerated influx of God's Light can give the appearance that things are getting worse, but nothing could be further from the Truth. That is an illusion. The Beings of Light have given us the following information because it is very important that we all understand what happens when we invoke the Light of God.

Once again, it is vital that we remember we are all One. There is no separation. In order for us to move forward in the Light, we must first transmute the human miscreations we created in the past. That means that anything that conflicts with the Light of God must come to the surface to be healed and transmuted back into its original perfection. This is what is meant by the statement "*All that is hidden must now be revealed.*"

Regardless of how deplorable our human miscreations are, the energy that comprises those gross mutations was originally pure Light from the Heart of God. You and I and every other person responsible for creating those miscreations must transmute that energy back into pure Light. This is true for every single human miscreation. Anything that is not reflecting the harmony and balance of the patterns of perfection in the Causal Body of God is a human miscreation. That includes poverty, disease, hatred, prejudice, corruption, greed, violence, war, religious fanaticism, abuse of power, and every other physical manifestation that is less than the perfection of Heaven on Earth.

I know this seems like a daunting responsibility, but Heaven on Earth is exactly what God and the Elemental Kingdom created for us in the beginning. We made a covenant with our Father-Mother God in order to be allowed to come to Earth to learn the lessons of cocreation. Our covenant was that we would use our gift of Life to maintain the pristine beauty of the Earth and to cocreate new patterns of perfection.

When we invoke the Light of God through our prayers, meditations, invocations, decrees, affirmations, or any other way, our Father-Mother God respond and the Light of God increases on Earth. This frequency of God's Infinite Perfection floods the planet and enters the core of purity in every atomic and subatomic particle and wave of Life.

Regardless of how dark or contaminated our human miscreations are, the energy within the core of that miscreation still pulsates with its original Divine Potential. That is true for every person, place, condition, or thing existing on this planet. For instance, in the core of every expression of poverty still pulsates the Divine Potential for God's Infinite Abundance; within the core of every facet of disease still pulsates the Divine Potential of vibrant health; within every manifestation of war is the Divine Potential of peace; within every electron of hatred is the Divine Potential of love. This is true for people as well. No matter how far a person has fallen or how depraved or degenerate he or she may seem, that person still has the full Divine Potential of a Beloved Child of God blazing in their Heart Flame.

The reason it sometimes appears as though things are getting worse after we invoke the Light of God is because of what happens when the Light enters the core of purity. When the Light of God enters the core of purity, it activates the original Divine Potential that is still encoded within that particle of Life. Everything that conflicts with that potential is then pushed to the surface to be healed and transmuted back into Light. This is a necessary part of the process that has to be successfully accomplished in order to clear the way for the tangible manifestation of the Divine Potential.

What this means very practically is that when we invoke prosperity, the Light of God enters the core of purity in every electron of energy in our lives that conflicts with prosperity. This Light activates the Divine Potential in that energy, which is God's Infinite Abundance. Then the vibration of God's Abundance pushes to the surface every thought, word, action, or feeling that is responsible for manifesting our poverty. As the patterns that created our poverty surface to be healed, it often looks like things are getting worse, but that is never the case.

This illusion is caused by the fact that we can easily see the patterns associated with our poverty that are being pushed to the surface to be healed. What we cannot see as easily, is the powerful Light of God that is pushing those distorted patterns to the surface in order to clear the way for our prosperity. With the limited perception of our fearful human egos, we end up focusing our attention on the surfacing patterns of poverty instead of the patterns for God's Infinite Abundance.

We create our Earthly experiences through our thoughts and feelings. If we focus on poverty, that is what we empower and sustain in our lives. It is just that simple. Through our lack of understanding, we have created a vicious circle for ourselves. That is why these *"end times"* have been referred to in many teachings as *"The time of screaming, and the gnashing of teeth."*

It is time for us to learn how to transmute the surfacing negativity in a more effective way, while staying focused on the positive things we are invoking. The Company of Heaven has given us guidance and wonderful tools that will help us to do just that. That information will be discussed later in the pages of this book. But first, let me share with you some of the miracles Lightworkers and the Company of Heaven cocreated after we began our ascent into the 4th Dimension.

# ASCENDING THROUGH
# THE DOORWAY OF 11:11

After the acceleration of energy, vibration, and consciousness, which took place within all Life during Harmonic Convergence, the Light of God rapidly increased on Earth. Humanity was awakening at an accelerated pace, and people everywhere were participating in activities of Light designed to heal the planet and shift Humanity's global perspective.

In spite of these selfless efforts, there were still masses of Humanity who were oblivious to what was occurring on Earth. These people were buried in the oppressive frequencies of their lives, and many of them were being totally manipulated by their human egos. It became clear to the Company of Heaven that there were many fallen souls who were so entangled with their human egos that they may not wake up in time to make the shift into the 5th Dimension with the rest of our Solar System. At the same time, there were millions of awakening Lightworkers who had great potential for raising their vibrations and transmuting their human miscreations in time for this glorious Ascension. The only solution seemed to be the creation of a second Earth.

The prophecies of old have talked about *"the New Earth, and the old Earth passing away,"* but this was a facet of the plan that every Lightworker was striving to avert. This plan would mean that those who were ready to Ascend into the 5th Dimension would be able to do so, but those who were not ready would be left behind. Nobody wanted that to happen, but it seemed as though the human egos of the recalcitrant souls were determined to block the Light and maintain control. This sad situation made the creation of a 4th-Dimensional Earth the only viable option.

Our Father-Mother God directed Alpha and Omega to fulfill this facet of the plan. They invoked the Mighty Elohim, who are the Builders of Form, and the members of the Elemental Kingdom who would be responsible for cocreating the 4th-Dimensional New Earth. The knowledge of this unfolding Divine Plan was projected into the mental strata of Earth, and awakened Lightworkers all over the planet volunteered to be the open door for this influx of Light.

A global activity of Light that was called *Ascending Through the Doorway of 11:11* was set into motion, and Lightworkers all over the world participated according to the inner guidance of their Solar Christ Presences. This event involved a rare window of opportunity that united Heaven and Earth for a six-month period. It began with a very powerful Solar Eclipse on July 11, 1991, and built in momentum until the completion of the global activity of Light on January 11, 1992.

That six-month period created a sacred space that allowed the Mighty Elohim and the Elemental Kingdom to cocreate the 4th-Dimensional New Earth. The two Earths existed in the same time and space, but they were vibrating at different frequencies. Humanity could freely move between the old Earth and the New Earth depending on what we chose to empower each day with our thoughts, feelings, words, and actions. Many Lightworkers chose to remain in the frequencies of the New Earth and did so by focusing on the patterns of perfection from the Causal Body of God. Many unawakened souls remained in the discordant frequencies of the old Earth, because they did not realize they had another option.

The Lightworkers knew there would come a time in the not-too-distant future when the New Earth would Ascend into the 5th Dimension, and the old Earth would be left behind. The souls left behind would be escorted back to Alpha and Omega, where they would have to wait in a state of limbo until the opportunity was presented for them to be reborn in another system. That system needed to be dense enough to withstand the human miscreations the souls would be bringing with them.

This scenario is what all of the Lightworkers had been trying to prevent. Even though we realized the chances were slim of reversing the direction the fallen souls were headed in, we did not want to give up on them. Lightworkers all over the world continued invoking the Light of God, and working tenaciously with the Company of Heaven to awaken these souls as quickly as possible.

## MAKING PEACE WITH THE ELEMENTAL KINGDOM

The potential was great that awakened Lightworkers would be able to move into the 5th Dimension, but that did not mean that our work was finished. We still had a long way to go before our physical, etheric, mental, and emotional bodies would be vibrating at a frequency that could withstand the 5th Dimension. This meant that we needed to make peace with our Body Elementals.

One of the most devastating results of our fall from Grace was the schism that was formed between Humanity and the Elemental Beings who had so selflessly volunteered to sustain our Earthly bodies in a state of youthful, vibrant health. In selfless service to Humanity, the Elemental Kingdom had also volunteered to sustain the body of Mother Earth in the pristine beauty of the Garden of Eden.

We lost the awareness of the Elemental Kingdom when our Crown Chakras closed and we no longer had contact with our Christ Selves. Since that time our egos have manipulated us into believing that the physical plane is all that exists and that the Earth is here for Humanity to use and abuse as we will. Our egos tricked us into believing that this planet is an inanimate object and that she is void of intelligence.

Our human egos took control of our Earthly bodies and decided that their sole purpose was to gratify our physical senses. Once this occurred, our Body Elementals were forced to outpicture the grotesque mutations of aging, disease, mental illness, deformities, and all of the degenerative diseases we have miscreated. Even death, as we know it now, is a human miscreation.

When our negative thoughtforms and feelings were projected onto the Elemental Beings sustaining the body of Mother Earth, we started experiencing inclement weather conditions, earthquakes, volcanos, hurricanes, tornados, floods, droughts, famines, plagues, pestilence, pollution of every conceivable kind, and everything else that is not reflecting the perfection of Heaven on Earth.

After the creation of the 4th-Dimensional New Earth, it was clear that the next phase of Humanity's healing process needed to be mending our rift with the Elemental Kingdom. The Company of Heaven was well aware of this need. As the statement from our Father-Mother God affirms, *"Before you have called, I have answered."*

A couple of years preceding our Ascension through the Doorway of 11:11, the Beings of Light projected a plan into the mental strata of Earth with the Divine Intent of accomplishing this mission. Lightworkers around the world responded. An activity of Light was unfolding that was designed to heal the schism between Humanity and the Elemental Kingdom. This event was the *First Earth Summit*, to be held in Rio de Janeiro, Brazil, June 1-14, 1992.

The First Earth Summit was an amazing event. For the first time ever, 176 world leaders came together for a common cause—the healing of the Earth. Each leader had his or her own agenda and ideas on how the healing would be accomplished, but the fact that all were in agreement that something needed to be done to heal the Earth was significant and unprecedented.

In addition to the world leaders, 40,000 individuals representing organizations committed to planetary healing and sustainable growth also traveled to Rio. These Lightworkers joined in consciousness with Lightworkers all over the world who were tuning in to this global event. Together we created a Chalice of Light that sent a beacon of hope to the Elemental Kingdom. This sacred gathering was the outer world demonstration the Elementals had been waiting for to prove that Humanity was worthy of regaining their trust, and that we were ready to reclaim our position as stewards of the Earth.

Our Mother God, the Holy Spirit, has always been the sustaining force behind the Elemental Kingdom. That is why we refer to Mother Nature and Mother Earth. Her Loving Presence was a critical factor in the healing that took place between Humanity and the Elemental Kingdom at the First Earth Summit.

On June 1, 1992, the Earth Summit began. The Lightworkers at the summit, and those tuning in from around the world, expanded our Chalice of Light until it enveloped the entire Planet Earth. This unified Cup of Consciousness created an open portal between Heaven and Earth. The Love of our Mother God flowed through this portal into the physical plane, and bathed Humanity and the Elemental Kingdom in its healing unguent.

For seven days Humanity and the Elemental Kingdom experienced the Love of our Mother God in ways that transcended the atrocities we had perpetrated on each other.

Through Divine Grace, the pain and suffering Humanity and the Elemental Kingdom had inflicted on each other was forgiven. The Elemental Kingdom agreed to establish a new covenant with Humanity.

June 7, 1992, was the day that is celebrated in the outer world as Pentecost. It was the midpoint of the Earth Summit, and the Love of our Mother God had been building to a tremendous crescendo. It was not by chance that the apex of the Earth Summit fell on the day that is dedicated to the Holy Spirit, the Divine Presence who sustains and nurtures the Elemental Kingdom. On that sacred and holy day, inner and outer world activities of Light took place at the Earth Summit that allowed Humanity and the Elemental Kingdom to integrate our Mother God's Love and to heal our separation.

Through the Solar Christ Presence of every man, woman, and child on Earth, a new covenant of Divine Love was formed between Humanity and the Elemental Kingdom. A new consciousness of trust and cooperation was established that will allow us to work together for the healing of Humanity's Earthly bodies and the bodies of Mother Earth. Instead of the cataclysmic Earth changes that had been prophesied, which were destined to result in the death of millions of people, the purging will now be done in a much gentler way.

The Earth is a living, breathing organism, and we have abused her terribly. In order for her to Ascend into the 5th Dimension, she will have to purge and cleanse herself. We will experience inclement weather conditions until the cleansing is complete; the difference is that now millions of people will not die in the process. There will be some loss of life, but it will be a minuscule fraction of what was originally predicted. The souls who leave the planet during this purging process, at some level have agreed to go through the experience. We are all going through the experiences that our

God Selves have agreed to go through. This is true regardless of how unaware we may be on a conscious level of the agreements we made with our Father-Mother God.

The new covenant between Humanity and the Elemental Kingdom healed the rift with our Body Elementals as well. Now our Body Elementals will work with us to reopen the Elemental Vortices in each of our bodies. Together we will prepare our physical, etheric, mental, and emotional bodies for the monumental changes that we must go through if we are going to be ready for our Ascension into the 5th Dimension.

As amazing as this may seem, we are transforming our bodies at a cellular level from carbon-based cells into crystalline-based cells. We are becoming 5th-Dimensional Solar Light Beings. Wow!

## REMOVING   THE   INTERFERENCE

Humanity's awakening accelerated after the healing with the Elemental Kingdom. People all over the world observed changes taking place in their lives, and they began asking questions. The heartfelt inquiries of thousands of people opened the door for our Solar Christ Presences to communicate with us in more tangible ways. As more people listened to *"the still small voice within,"* our Mother God's Love expanded exponentially through all Life.

The influx of our Mother God's Love was a blessing to Humanity and the Elemental Kingdom, but it created more fear and resistance in our human egos. This fragmented aspect of our personality did not understand that it was being given the opportunity to be transformed and loved into the Light. It thought it was being destroyed. This fear motivated our human egos to act out in more volatile ways. The more willing our egos were to add to the chaos of the world, the more they became the pawns of the forces of imbalance who still had some access to the Earth.

After the sinking of Lemuria and Atlantis, the vast majority of our fallen sisters and brothers, who had come from outside of the Solar System of Alpha and Omega to wreak havoc on the Earth, were forced to leave. But there were some who were still able to interact adversely with our human egos. These were the souls who had enticed our sisters and brothers on the other 143 planets in this system to partake of the tree of knowledge of good and evil. They were the same souls who after the fall changed our mission from a school of cocreation to a school of duality and separation.

Lightworkers were very aware of this outside interference. As the Light of God increased on Earth, reports of psychic attacks, alien abductions, possessions, and every other bizarre phenomenon increased as well. Many of these perceived experiences were just projected thoughtforms from the psychic-astral plane, but some of them were actual interference from our nefarious sisters and brothers.

These fallen souls had absolutely no power over the Light, so the people who were most vulnerable to their negative influence were the souls who were stuck in the 3rd-Dimensional frequencies of the old Earth. These were the very people the Lightworkers were striving to awaken in time to make the shift into the 5th Dimension.

For several years Lightworkers all over the world participated in myriad activities of Light that raised the energy, vibration, and consciousness of every facet of Life on the Earth. The Lightworkers knew the Truth within the statement, *"As I AM lifted up, ALL Life is lifted up with me."* We understood that the only way the souls outside of our system, who were wreaking havoc on the planet, could be removed from the Earth was for us to love them into the Light.

Finally, in 1996, the love pouring through the Heart Flames of the Lightworkers reached a powerful enough frequency to cut Humanity free from the interference of the forces of imbalance. In unison with the Company of Heaven, our Solar Christ Presences created a forcefield of Divine Love powerful enough to stir the Divinity within the hearts of these fallen souls. As their hearts began to soften, they were magnetized into our forcefield of Divine Love. Once they willingly entered this sacred space and were bathed in the frequencies of our Mother God's Love, they relaxed their resolve to oppose the Light. This gave Archangel Michael permission to intervene in an unprecedented way.

In a wondrous activity of Light involving the entire Company of Heaven and Lightworkers all over the world, Archangel Michael encapsulated these souls in a forcefield of Light called *"The Ring Pass Not of God's First Cause of Perfection."* This is a 5th-Dimensional circle of white lightning that prevents anything that is not of the Light from entering or leaving the circle. Once the souls were encapsulated in this forcefield of Divine Light, they realized that their reign of terror was over. Archangel Michael then escorted the fallen souls into the Temples of Divine Grace and Reverence for All Life in the inner planes.

After being bathed for a period of time in the supreme Light and Truth within these sacred Temples, the wayward souls voluntarily surrendered to the Divinity within their own Heart Flames. They agreed to make amends for their karmic liabilities and to do whatever was necessary in order to move into the Light. After their process of redemption was complete, Archangel Michael escorted the souls back to the Heart of our Father-Mother

God. In Divine Timing, they will be reinstated to their original Divine Intent as Sons and Daughters of God.

It is difficult for us to comprehend the magnitude of what was victoriously accomplished through this unified effort of Lightworkers and the Beings of Light, but that event forever changed Humanity's struggle. The souls who had been wreaking havoc in the lives of the Sons and Daughters of God throughout the Universe for millions of years had been removed from the Earth and loved into the Light. These souls will never again be in a position to harm any facet of Life.

Now the only battle Humanity has left is the inner battle with our human egos. In the past that was a gargantuan struggle, but we were not aware of the multifaceted and multidimensional aspects of our own Divinity. Now that we realize we are Sons and Daughters of God, we can take our power back. When we consciously choose to take back the power our human egos usurped from our God Selves, the battle with our human egos will be a piece of cake. This terrified, fragmented aspect of our personality is like a wayward child who just needs to be held and loved until it feels safe enough to let go of its control of our lives. When that happens, our human egos will be loved free and transformed into Light.

All of the maladies being perpetuated on Earth at this time are the result of our out-of-control human egos. Imagine the transfiguration that will take place when every man, woman, and child relinquishes control of his or her life to the Divinity pulsating in their hearts. This may seem like an impossible dream, but it is not. In fact, that transfiguration is much closer than it seems from outer appearances.

# TRANSFIGURING DIVINE LOVE

After the forces of imbalance were removed from the Earth, Humanity began to awaken at an even faster pace. The information pouring into the mental strata of Earth through the window of the dawning New Age was being received by people in all walks of life. If one person wasn't presenting the information in a way you could relate to, there were hundreds of other people saying the same thing in slightly different ways. Regardless of how the information was being perceived, everyone realized that something unique was happening. Some people had wonderful expectations and others were terrified by reports of gloom and doom, but they all agreed the winds of change were blowing on this planet.

The fear and the misinformation about Y2K and the shift into the new millennium provided the Lightworkers with the opportunity to redouble our efforts. Millions of Lightworkers around the world invoked the Light of God in ways that transcended Humanity's fears. Light is infinitely more powerful than fear and the fragmented thoughtforms of our human egos, so when the year 2000 arrived, the Light prevailed. The Earth and all her Life were catapulted up the Spiral of Evolution a quantum leap. This shift raised the New Earth into higher frequencies of the 4th Dimension, which created a greater distance for our sisters and brothers on the old Earth to overcome.

The Lightworkers were very aware that we needed more help if our sisters and brothers on the old Earth were going to awaken in time. In spite of the valiant efforts being made by millions of people all over the world, there were still millions of people who were in danger of not waking up in time to make the shift into the 5th Dimension.

Lightworkers appealed to Alpha and Omega and invoked the Solar Christ Presences of every man, woman, and child on both the New and the old Earths. We invoked assistance from our Father-Mother God and the Beings of Light throughout the Universe. Everyone responded. Not a single Son or Daughter of God throughout the whole of Creation ignored the heartfelt plea of the Lightworkers embodied on Earth. With that Universal outpouring of Divine Love, Alpha and Omega initiated a plan that they said would be...

*"Humanity's last, best hope of choosing to move into the Light before the Shift of the Ages."*

This plan involved the activation of the most powerful frequency of Divine Love in all Creation. This was the *Flame of Transfiguring Divine Love*. This Sacred Fire had been resting in dormancy in the Causal Body of God, awaiting the Cosmic Moment when the collective body of the Sons and Daughters of God, throughout the entire Universe, would join their Heart Flames and call it into action.

Alpha and Omega said that the reason the Flame of Transfiguring Divine Love was considered the last, best hope to awaken our sisters and brothers is because of its unique properties. This Sacred Fire is a beautiful deep rose colored flame with an aquamarine aura of Divine Clarity. Pulsating in the center of the flame is an opalescent Sun of Transfiguration. Alpha and Omega revealed that there is a Divine Intelligence within this Sacred Fire that exposes anything that is not of the Light.

Once the Flame of Transfiguring Divine Love is anchored in the Immortal Victorious Threefold Flame in a person's heart, the Divine Intelligence within that flame begins to expose the distorted beliefs and manipulations of the human ego. The person will have the opportunity to perceive Truth in a new way. Then he or she can make the conscious decision to change their behavior patterns in a more informed way. The person still has free will, of course, but when he or she sees a new perspective that exposes the flawed thinking of the human ego, positive choices will be made much more easily.

In January 2001, the Company of Heaven indicated that several activities of Light would have to take place in order to expand Humanity's Threefold Flame enough to withstand the frequencies of the Flame of Transfiguring Divine Love. If all went well, this Sacred Fire would be anchored in the Heart Flame of every man., woman, and child during the 14th anniversary of Harmonic Convergence in August 2001.

Lightworkers joined with the Company of Heaven and participated in one activity of Light after another. Day by day the Threefold Flame within every person on Earth was expanded by his or her Solar Christ Presence the maximum that Cosmic Law would allow. When the 14th anniversary of Harmonic Convergence arrived, all was in readiness. In an unprecedented invocation, the Sons and Daughters of God throughout the whole of Creation called the Flame of Transfiguring Divine Love into action. On the Holy Breath of God, this Sacred Flame was securely anchored in every person's Heart Flame.

Once that was successfully accomplished, the Divine Intelligence within this Sacred Fire began pushing to the surface every distorted belief and behavior pattern of Humanity's human egos. Many people abiding on the old Earth began to awaken. They realized that, for some unknown reason, they were able to *"see with new eyes, and hear with new ears."* They were able to look at old problems and perceive new, viable solutions that enhanced their lives and added to the Light of the world.

There were others who were being so manipulated by their terrified human egos that they could not perceive the Light of Divine Intelligence within the Flame of Transfiguring Divine Love. All they could see was the surfacing patterns of their human miscreations. Some of them latched onto these deplorable human miscreations and brought them into manifestation.

On September 11, 2001, we witnessed an example of the barbaric lengths to which Humanity's human egos will go in order to maintain control of our lives. I know there is a lot of controversy over what really happened on 9-11, and who was responsible. Hopefully, the Truth will be revealed one day. But for our purposes here, the Beings of Light want us to pay attention to the miscreations of our human egos that were exposed in that event. Almost everything that conflicts with our Father God's Divine Power, our Mother God's Divine Love, and the Reverence for Life was pushed to the surface during the events of 9-11.

We were told that the events of 9-11 were orchestrated by men who were religious extremists. Men who believe that women should be controlled and oppressed; and that they have the right to kill anyone who disagrees with their beliefs. Two planes flew into the towers of the World Trade Center, which represented the monetary system and the world's economy. Another plane flew into the Pentagon, which represents the military and the war machine. And finally, the fourth plane was intended to fly into the Capitol Building, which represents government.

It is interesting to observe that almost every abuse of power our human egos have used to manipulate us for aeons of time was exposed in the events of September 11, 2001:

1. The abuse of our MASCULINE POWER
2. The abuse of WOMEN
3. The abuse of RELIGION

4. The abuse of MONEY
5. The WAR MACHINE
6. The abuse of GOVERNMENT
7. Willingness to LIE, CHEAT, STEAL, KILL

Our human egos' attempts to block the expansion of Transfiguring Divine Love in the hearts of Humanity failed. When the news of the attacks on America started spreading around the world, the openhearted response was awe-inspiring. The leaders of the free world reacted by expressing their solidarity with the United States. Lightworkers all over the world joined their hearts and prayers. We invoked calm, and asked people around the world to hold the Light. The love and compassion that flowed through the newly-activated Flame of Transfiguring Divine Love in every Heart Flame opened Humanity's Heart Chakras further, which allowed the Love of our Mother God to have greater access to the planet.

For several weeks the Flame of Transfiguring Divine Love flowed unimpeded through the surfacing patterns of our human egos' miscreations. This moved the old Earth closer to the New Earth and created a more hopeful potential for our sisters and brothers to awaken.

It wasn't long before our human egos seemed to gain the upper hand again. From outer appearances it looked like every bit of compassion and good will was being squandered by the human miscreations of war, but that was not the case. The Beings of Light want to remind us that the people who are involved in the atrocities appearing on the screen of Life are a minuscule fraction of the almost 7 billion people abiding on this planet. There are *billions* of people who turn their attention to a higher power and invoke the Light of God every single day.

These people are Lightworkers, and they are adding to the Light of the world. Even though many of them are not consciously aware of the bigger picture happening on this planet, their God Selves are certainly aware. This aspect of their Divinity is able to intervene in their lives in ways that have not been possible since our fall from Grace millions of years ago. Through the Grace of God, miracles are happening.

## A MIRACLE

Once the Flame of Transfiguring Divine Love was anchored in every person's Heart Flame, it blazed in, through, and around the lives and experiences of each and every one of us. Daily and hourly, with every breath we took, the gifts of this Sacred Fire built in momentum. The Divine Intelligence within the flame continued the process of exposing the distorted perceptions of our human egos, which gave us the opportunity to make more life-enhancing choices.

After several months of this cleansing process, a shift took place within the mass consciousness of Humanity. This dramatic change inspired the Lightworkers to increase our efforts. With the help of the Company of Heaven, we projected more Light into the Heart Flames of the Solar Christ Presences of the souls who were stuck in the old Earth. As more Light flooded into the old Earth, the hearts of even the most resistant souls began to soften. This opened the door for a glorious miracle that transcended the greatest expectations of the Company of Heaven.

In August 2002, during an activity of Light that was taking place on the 15th anniversary of Harmonic Convergence, Heaven and Earth came together on behalf of every man, woman, and child who was at risk of not awakening in time to make the shift into the 5th Dimension. In a rare moment of unparalleled Divine

Grace, Alpha and Omega magnetized into the Heart of the Central Sun every person on Earth who had not yet chosen to move forward in the Light. This event took place for every person, in their finer bodies, as they slept at night.

Once these souls entered the Heart of the Central Sun, an extremely rare event took place. For one Cosmic Instant, Alpha and Omega suspended their free will. During that instant, the souls were compelled to peer into the Mirror of Life and perceive their own Divinity. For many of them it had been aeons of time since they had the slightest inkling that they were a Son or Daughter of God. Once they saw the Truth of their own Divinity, their free will was restored. Then Alpha and Omega gave them each one last chance to choose whether or not they were willing to do what was necessary in order to make their Ascension into the 5th Dimension.

The souls were shown their human miscreations and the retributions they would have to make in order to transmute those distorted patterns back into Light. They understood that the work they needed to do for their redemption was great, and that the time for them to accomplish that feat was short. But to the astonishment of even Alpha and Omega, every single fallen soul made the choice to do what is necessary for him or her to make the shift into the 5th Dimension. *This was a miracle!*

It meant that no one would be left behind. Every person evolving on Earth was going to make the shift into the 5th Dimension. This is what the Lightworkers had been dedicating our lives to for millennia. Now, in the 11th hour, VICTORY IS OURS! And the Heavens are rejoicing.

## THE TWO EARTHS BECOME ONE

The fact that every single person on Earth made the choice to move into the 5th Dimension was a miracle of unfathomable proportions, but it meant that our work as Lightworkers would be intensified a thousand fold. Since even the most recalcitrant souls had chosen to move into the Light, there was no longer a need for two Earths. That meant that all of the human miscreations that were initially going to be left behind with the fallen souls when the old Earth passed away, now had to be brought into the 4th-Dimensional New Earth. This was necessary in order for the souls to be able to transmute those gross mutations into Light. It is important for all of us to understand that this miracle would not have been allowed if it was going to cause the downfall of the awakening souls on the planet. Our Father-Mother God and the Company of Heaven allowed this to happen, because they clearly perceived the tenacity of the Lightworkers and our willingness to assist our sisters and brothers until they can raise their heads above the mud puddle of their miscreations enough to see the Light.

The 4th-Dimensional Solar Christ Presences of the souls on the old Earth began the process of preparing their Earthly bodies to withstand the frequencies of the 4th Dimension. This was done by gently increasing the frequency of Light flowing through their Solar Spine and Chakras. As their vibrations increased, the souls' human egos lost the ability to have such a paralyzing grip on their Earthly bodies. This enabled the souls' Solar Christ Presences to have a greater influence in their lives.

This was very important, because even though the souls had agreed to do whatever was necessary to move into the 5th Dimension, that commitment was made in the inner realms while they were in their finer bodies. Consequently, most of these souls did not have a conscious memory of their agreement. That did not change the fact that the choice was made, it just made it more difficult for these souls to understand why their human miscreations were surfacing at such an accelerated pace. The more influence their Solar Christ Presences had in their lives, the greater the chances were that they would not latch onto these surfacing miscreations and bring them into manifestation.

In Divine Timing, Alpha and Omega sounded a Cosmic Tone and the Mighty Elohim Inbreathed the old Earth into the frequencies of the New Earth. On the Holy Breath of God, the two Earths merged and became One. The God Victorious accomplishment of this event was celebrated throughout the Universe. In deepest gratitude the Legions of Light throughout Infinity agreed to intensify the assistance they were giving to the Lightworkers on Earth. A new Divine Plan was set into motion to prepare *every* evolving soul for the impending global shift of consciousness.

# CHAPTER NINE

# THE  CONTINGENCY  PLAN

When the two Earths became One, the game plan for planet Earth changed dramatically. In 2003, a new contingency plan was initiated by our Father-Mother God that required Lightworkers to invest even more of our Lifeforce to help our sisters and brothers awaken. Of course, our involvement in this new plan had to be our free-will choice.

Every Lightworker on the planet was taken into the Heart of God and given the opportunity to renew the vows we took prior to this embodiment. Then we were asked by our omniscient, omnipresent, omnipotent Father-Mother God—All That Is—if we would be willing to dedicate ourselves to a higher level of Divine Service on behalf of Humanity and all Life on this blessed planet. This opportunity occurred for each of us, in our finer bodies, as we slept at night.

Knowing the miracles that had already taken place, the vast majority of Lightworkers enthusiastically volunteered to increase the Lightwork we were doing to help the Earth and all her Life to Ascend into the 5th Dimension. We agreed to pay attention and to respond to the opportunities that would allow us to most effectively add to the Light of the world. Even though many Lightworkers may not consciously remember this new agreement, our decisions are recorded in our etheric bodies, and our God Selves will push them to the surface whenever we need encouragement or renewed confidence. Listen to your heart. This Truth will surface as an *inner knowing*.

Once the Lightworkers agreed to become active participants in the contingency plan, our Father-Mother God issued a Cosmic Dispensation to assist us in our selfless efforts to help Humanity, and all Life. This dispensation gave the Company of Heaven permission to amplify our Lightwork one thousandfold when we are invoking the Light by ourselves. This means that when we are alone, every time we invoke the Light in any way, there are the equivalent of 1,000 Beings of Light praying with us. That is a precious gift of Divine Grace.

However, due to the urgency of the hour, Lightworkers are being encouraged to join together for our Lightwork. When we join with other Lightworkers in groups and in consciousness for global meditations, this merciful dispensation is greatly expanded. The Company of Heaven has been given permission to amplify our group efforts A THOUSAND TIMES A THOUSAND FOLD. Imagine! This exponential expansion of Light is one of the main reasons that the victory of Earth's Ascension into the 5th Dimension is assured. This does not mean our work is finished. It means it is time for all of us to join together, and to work our tails off.

With this Cosmic Dispensation, the Company of Heaven and embodied Lightworkers joined forces and gave us new avenues of communication. The Internet exploded onto the screen of Life and offered new and innovative ways for Lightworkers around the world to connect with each other. Global meditations and activities of Light allowed literally millions of Lightworkers to join together in one-pointed consciousness as we invoked the Light of God on behalf of all Life on Earth. Each of these global activities of Light was expanded a thousand times a thousandfold by the Company of Heaven.

Things began shifting in our lives, and the work of Lightworkers all over the world took a quantum leap in new, diverse directions. We integrated the changes in our spiritual paths and fine-tuned our renewed commitment and dedication to our spiritual work. We accepted opportunities that were presented to us, and day by day, millions of Lightworkers increased the Light we were adding to the world.

In the midst of our greatly accelerated Lightwork, the Beings of Light revealed to us that *2003* was the year in which the Cosmic Alignment would take place that would trigger the initial impulse of Humanity's Ascension into the 5th Dimension. This was the Inbreath of our Father-Mother God, *the Shift of the Ages*, for which Humanity had been preparing for more than 500 years.

This revelation caught every Lightworker by surprise. We knew the shift was imminent, but we were focused on the year *2012*. This was the year that had been given to the world by the Mayans and other indigenous peoples. We asked the Beings of Light for clarity, and we were given the following information.

The Beings of Light in the Realms of Illumined Truth said there were several factors involving what seemed to be a change in the date for the Shift of the Ages. All of the factors involve Humanity's free-will choices and the fact that we are cocreating the experiences taking place on Earth. We are not just observers waiting for something to happen.

One of the factors is that the calendar the Mayans used is different from the calendar we use today. The changes that were made in our calendar caused the discrepancy between the Mayan year 2012 and the Gregorian year 2003. Another factor is due to the tremendous influx of God's Light. This is causing the vibratory rate of the planet to increase on a daily basis. We are moving closer to the frequencies of the timeless, spaceless 5th Dimension, so everything is being accelerated. Even time is going faster.

In spite of any confusion, the Beings of Light want us to understand that our Ascension into the 5th Dimension is a process that we are cocreating. It is not an event that will occur in one day through outside influences. As we invoke the Light of God each day, we need to stay focused in the Eternal Moment of Now. We must not allow our human egos to be distracted with the past or the future.

When the Lightworkers realized that the Shift of the Ages would begin in 2003, we understood *"the urgency of the hour"* that the Beings of Light kept referring to as they inspired us to keep on keeping on. In August 2001, the Flame of Transfiguring Divine Love was anchored in every person's Heart Flame. This was the Sacred Fire that Alpha and Omega said would be the fallen soul's last, best hope of choosing to move into the Light in time for the shift. In August 2002, Alpha and Omega gave the fallen souls one last chance to choose to move into the Light. Through an unprecedented act of Divine Grace, every one of those souls made the choice to move into the 5th Dimension. Then the two Earths merged and became One in the 4th Dimension. After that event was successfully accomplished, the Solar Christ Presence of every man, woman, and child began the process of accelerating the energy, vibration, and consciousness of our Earthly bodies, so we could withstand the Ascension into the 5th Dimension. If we had known how close the Shift of the Ages was, we would probably have panicked and allowed ourselves to become overwhelmed. Mercifully, we did not realize just how urgent the hour was.

If you ever feel abandoned or alone, I want you to reread the previous paragraph. You will clearly see how very loved you are, and you will know what awesome assistance has been administered on your behalf by the Legions of Light throughout Infinity.

In January 2003, Lightworkers began participating in activities of Light to prepare Humanity for the upcoming Shift of the Ages. Each of these global events was designed to raise the vibrations of our Earthly bodies the maximum that Cosmic Law would allow. The Divine Intent was for Humanity to make the shift into the initial impulse of the 5th Dimension as painlessly as possible.

This process was catapulted to the next level during two very powerful Eclipses. The first was a Lunar Eclipse on May 15, 2003, and the second was a Solar Eclipse on May 31, 2003. During the days between the two Eclipses, a portal was opened into the 5th Dimension. In that Cosmic Moment, the Company of Heaven and Humanity's I AM Presences Inbreathed our Solar Christ Presences and our 4th-Dimensional Solar Spines and Chakras through the open door into the 5th Dimension.

During that momentous event, Humanity's Solar Christ Presences and our 4th-Dimensional Solar Spines and Chakras merged and became One with our I AM Presences and our 5th-Dimensional Solar Spines and Chakras. This was a critical step in order for Humanity to be able to withstand the frequencies of the 5th Dimension. This event took place within every man, woman, and child on Earth in perfect alignment with our Divine Plans and our highest good.

The various aspects of our Divinity have now merged into one magnificent Being of Light. This simplifies everything. Now our Planetary Christ Self, our Solar Christ Presence, and our I AM Presence are One. And our sevenfold Planetary Spine, our twelvefold 4th-Dimensional Solar Spine, and our twelvefold 5th-Dimensional Solar Spine are also One. This means that in order for us to connect with ALL of the aspects of our Divinity, even our Causal Bodies and our White Fire Beings, *all we need to do now is invoke our I AM Presence.*

With our Ascension into the frequencies of our 5th-Dimensional Solar Spine, our I AM Presence is no longer vibrating at a frequency beyond the reach of our physical, etheric, mental, and emotional bodies. Our I AM Presence is now able to integrate into these bodies at a cellular level. This is happening daily and hourly within each and every one of us. When this process is complete, we will have transformed our bodies from carbon-based cells to crystalline-based cells. Our Earthly bodies are becoming Solar Light Bodies.

The twelve Solar Chakras in our 5th-Dimensional Solar Spines are unique and radiate Light in ways that we have not experienced in the past. Each 5th-Dimensional Solar Chakra is a sphere of Light that radiates in every direction like a blazing Sun. All twelve of the Solar Aspects of Deity—the Circle of the Sacred Twelve—pulsates through each of the Chakras all of the time.

Even though all of the Solar Aspects of Deity pulsate through all of our Solar Chakras simultaneously, we have the ability to invoke them one at a time. If we want to amplify one of the Aspects of Deity for a particular reason or in a particular situation, we simply ask our I AM Presence to increase that particular Aspect of Deity through our Chakras.

For instance, if we want to increase healing, we ask our I AM Presence to amplify the 5th Solar Aspect of Healing. The emerald green Light instantly expands through all twelve Solar Chakras simultaneously transforming each one into a resplendent emerald green Sun of Healing. If we want to increase love, we ask our I AM Presence to amplify the 3rd Solar Aspect of Divine Love, and the crystalline pink Light begins to blaze through all of our Chakras until each one becomes a pink Sun of Divine Love.

Our I AM Presence always monitors the situation, and when the appropriate amount of healing or love has been projected, the Circle of the Sacred Twelve returns to perfect balance in each Chakra. We can amplify one or more Aspects of Deity through our 5th-Dimensional Solar Chakras any time we want to, and we can do it as often as we like according to the need of the hour and our service to the Light.

## OUR MOTHER GOD
## RETURNS TO EARTH

There was one more crucial facet of the unfolding Divine Plan that had to be successfully accomplished if the masses of Humanity were going to make it through the Shift of the Ages. This involved *the permanent return of our Mother God*. This wondrous event could occur only if Humanity's 5th-Dimensional Solar Heart Chakras were open to full breadth. We were told by the Company of Heaven that this facet of the plan would take place during the 16th anniversary of Harmonic Convergence, in August 2003, and that it would involve the unified efforts of embodied Lightworkers and the entire Company of Heaven.

Because of the recent activities of Light that had been successfully accomplished, the I AM Presences of both the Lightworkers and the masses of Humanity were able to intervene in this activity in unprecedented ways. For this event, Lightworkers around the world invoked the Transfiguring Divine Love of our Mother God and breathed this gift of the Holy Spirit into every person's Heart Flame. When the frequencies of our Mother God's Love merged with our Immortal Victorious Threefold Flames, the Divinity within our hearts expanded through our 5th-Dimensional Solar Heart Chakras and opened them to full breadth. Our I AM Presences took full dominion of our open Heart Chakras and held the sacred space for the return of our Mother God.

When all was in readiness, Archangel Gabriel sounded his mighty Trumpet announcing the return of our Mother God. Suddenly, waves of the most exquisite frequencies of Transfiguring Divine Love began flowing from the core of Creation into the Heart of our Mother God. She absorbed the sacred essence into her Heart Flame and then breathed the Breath of the Holy Spirit into the Heart Flame of every man, woman, and child evolving on Earth. Our Mother God then projected her luminous Presence into every Heart Chakra and securely anchored her Divine Presence within every Heart Flame.

*Our Mother God has returned to Earth, and she is now tangibly present in every person's Heart Flame.*

With the return of our Mother God, the Divine Masculine and Feminine were balanced within every Heart Flame. Humanity is now realigning with the Truth and inner knowing of what the Love of our Mother God really means in relation to our very existence.

So much has been written about love that it has almost become a platitude, but the Transfiguring Divine Love of our Mother God is the mightiest force in the Universe. It is the vibration from which we were born out of the Heart of God and the vibration through which we must evolve and Ascend back into the Heart of God. The Love of our Mother God has no bonds, no barriers, and no conditions. Within the infinite power of our Mother's Love there is no pain or sorrow, no lack or limitation. Her Love contains within its essence the full potential to rise above all human conditions, all self-inflicted suffering, all manner of chaos, confusion, hopelessness, and despair.

Our Mother God's Love heals the illusion of separation. It rejuvenates, revitalizes and makes whole all it embraces. It is the single greatest source of forgiveness, and it reverberates with the full-gathered momentum of our eternal freedom. Her Love is the foundation of Creation and the balance of the One. It is the indivisible, unchanging ecstasy that allows us to know Love in all things. When we experience the Love of our Mother God, we understand that we are all One. Whether we are a person, a magnificent Sun, or a blade of grass, the all-encompassing Light of our Mother's Love unites us in the Body of God.

As our Mother God reclaims this Earth and once again anoints Humanity with the Eternal Light of Divine Love, we experience true peace. Her Love is now resonating in the core of our Beings; it is not outside of us. We no longer need to seek the Divine Feminine from afar; we need to merely accept that our Mother God has returned, and that she is now abiding within our Heart Flames. Her Love is pulsating within the silent rhythm of every heartbeat, every breath. It is the universal language now speaking to all Humanity through our gift of Life. As we listen in the silence of our hearts, we hear the tones and whisperings of Love inspired by the wonder of nature and the Music of the Spheres.

Our Mother God is now reestablishing her covenant of Love with the Children of Earth, which will enhance our ability to once and for all accept the gift of God's Abundance. Through this covenant, the supply of all good things will forever and ever flood into the hands and use of the Sons and Daughters of God. The glory of God's Abundance will be a manifest reality not only in this moment, but far beyond Earth and time into Eternity.

The effulgence of our newly balanced Heart Flames is creating an environment of Love and upliftment around each of us. When we turn our attention to the balanced expression of our Father-Mother God within our hearts, the illusion of separation is shattered. Our hearts are unified, and we once again experience the bliss of knowing we are One, and that Love is all there is. This knowing evokes from within the deepest recesses of our Beings a celestial song of thanksgiving and a reverent feeling of Divine Gratitude. Every sunrise we see, every flower that shares its perfume with us, every friend and loved one who warms our heart is a gift of our Mother God's sustaining Love. These sacred gifts inspire our perpetual adoration to the Cosmic I AM, All That Is.

Our Mother God has placed us within a mantle of her Love, and our nervous systems are being recalibrated to withstand the highest frequencies of the Divine Feminine. This mantle of Love will help to transform each of us into conscious, self-generating centers of Light and Love. The tremendous impetus and magnetic pull of our Mother's Love now flowing through our Heart Flames are stirring the souls of Humanity. The invisible and resistless power of this Love is piercing into the sleeping spiritual brain centers of every member of the Human race and accelerating the awakening of every Human Being.

We now, as never before, have the ability to merge our personal service to Life with God's service to Life for the highest good of all concerned. Our Mother God's radiant, universal Love is pouring through all of us without designating favor to a particular person, place, condition or thing. Her Love is giving a healing, impersonal benediction to every particle of Life.

The power and magnetic Love of the Divine Feminine is blessing all Life with an equal opportunity to respond. Every evolving soul is being given both the blessing and the responsibility of becoming an open door for our Mother God's exquisite Love. Every Human Being now has the opportunity to become an instrument of God vested with the power to lift the feelings of all with whom we come in contact. This will be accomplished not through our human will, but through the balanced power of the Flame of Divinity now blazing in our hearts.

When we agree to become a magnetic force of Divine Love, we draw to ourselves the loving support we need from those who are aligned with, and will assist us with, our Divine Missions. This occurs not because of allegiance to a particular personality, but because of the affinity of our soul's Light with the particular facet of the Divine Plan.

As we expand our service to Life, we must reach up in consciousness and tap into the sacred knowledge and wisdom that will teach us how to effectively utilize the frequencies of Divine Love from our Mother God. Her Love is a priceless gift that is now freely flowing through every Heart Flame. The more we understand about the power and might of this majestic force, the more effective we will be in assimilating it into our life experiences.

With the God-Victorious return of our Mother God, everything was in place for the Shift of the Ages.

## HARMONIC   CONCORDANCE

The initial impulse of the Shift of the Ages took place during a global activity of Light that was referred to as *Harmonic Concordance*. This event was considered the 2nd wave of Harmonic Convergence, and it involved the conscious participation of millions of Lightworkers. People all over the world responded to their hearts' call and traveled to sacred sites and power points along the meridians of Earth's crystal grid system. This time, the energies anchored in the Heart Flames of the Lightworkers through the acupuncture points of the planet would secure the Earth and all her Life in the initial frequencies of the 5th Dimension.

This event occurred between two very powerful Eclipses in November 2003. The first was a Lunar Eclipse on November 8th, and the second was a Solar Eclipse on November

23rd. These Eclipses coincided with a rare celestial alignment that opened a portal of Divine Consciousness which extended from the Core of Creation into the Sun of Even Pressure in the heart of Mother Earth. During that rare alignment, our Father-Mother God flooded the Earth with their newly balanced *Violet Flame of God's Infinite Perfection*. This balanced frequency of our God Parent's Love and Power had not been available on Earth since our Mother God was forced to withdraw her Love after our fall from Grace aeons ago.

The Violet Flame of God's Infinite Perfection entered the core of purity in every electron of precious Life energy and activated the original Divine Potential within every particle of Life on Earth. As the Divine Potential expanded through every atomic and subatomic particle and wave of Life, everything that conflicted with that Divine Potential was pushed to the surface to be transmuted into Light.

Each of our I AM Presences participated in this wondrous opportunity by reaching back through all of our etheric records and memories. Myriad lifetimes worth of our human miscreations were pushed to the surface to be transmuted into Light. As the Violet Flame blazed in, through, and around every facet of Life, it created the most intensified purging and cleansing of Humanity's miscreations that Cosmic Law would allow.

This powerful influx of the Violet Flame from our Father-Mother God transmuted the majority of horrific human miscreations from the old Earth. This gift of Divine Grace paved the way for Humanity's remaining human miscreations and the negative things that our human egos were still manifesting, to be pushed to the surface more quickly. From outer appearances the surfacing negativity looked pretty much the same, but that was an illusion. In reality, thousands of lifetimes of Humanity's miscreations were purged and transmuted into Light during that Cosmic Moment.

This amazing cleansing lifted every man, woman, and child on Earth into more rarified frequencies of Light than we had ever experienced. This was the final step of preparation that Humanity needed in order to withstand the initial frequencies of the 5th Dimension. Once the purging was complete, the frequencies of the 5th Dimension were secured in every Heart Flame. Then our I AM Presences expanded that Light and anchored it in the core of purity within every electron of precious Life energy on Earth. This allowed Humanity to integrate higher levels of Divine Consciousness than we had ever known.

This was what every Lightworker had been working toward for thousands of lifetimes. This was just the beginning of our Ascension into the 5th Dimension, but the miracle was that *every person* evolving on Earth successfully made the shift. Now we have to join together and work with every fiber of our Beings to transmute the remaining human miscreations that are surfacing in the physical plane. Only then, will we complete our Ascension into the 5th-Dimensional Realms of Light with the rest of our Solar System.

Every man, woman, and child on Earth was allowed to make this shift, in spite of the fact that many are still very much asleep and their human egos are wreaking havoc all over the planet. The reason for this unprecedented act of Divine Grace is because our Father-Mother God know that the Lightworkers embodied on Earth are dedicated beyond measure. We have volunteered to hold the sacred space for our sisters and brothers until their human egos are loved into the Light and their I AM Presences take dominion of their lives. *We are our brothers' and sisters' keepers*. This is not a lofty platitude, this is a profound responsibility. Without a single doubt, we are going to do whatever is necessary to fulfill our part of this unique experiment.

For just a moment, go within to the Divinity of your Heart Flame. Feel our Father-Mother God and the entire Company of Heaven embracing *you* in an infinite flow of Divine Love and Gratitude. On behalf of all Life evolving on this planet, I want to thank you from the deepest recesses of my heart for volunteering to come to Earth during this Cosmic Moment and for your willingness to selflessly add to the Light of the world. You are a gift to all Life on this planet, and you are loved beyond your knowing.

## STAY FOCUSED ON THE LIGHT

*Oh, Father-Mother God, I invoke the full momentum of Your Divine Light and Love.*
*In deep humility and gratitude, I consecrate every facet of my Being to be the open door for this influx of Light.*

*I AM a Cup, a Holy Grail, through which the Light and Love of God are now flowing to bless ALL Life on Earth. Through the unspeakable power of God's Light and Love, every man, woman, and child comprehends the Truth that all Life is interconnected, interrelated and interdependent. A renewed sense of Oneness and Reverence for ALL Life now flows through each Heart Flame.*

*Every person knows—I AM my mighty I AM Presence.*
*I AM One with the Divine Heart and Mind of God.*
*I AM One with the I AM Presence of all Humanity.*
*I AM One with the Elemental Kingdom and Mother Earth.*
*I AM One with the Angelic Kingdom, and I AM One with ALL of the Beings of Light throughout Infinity.*

*Through this knowing, every person is raised into a higher
level of consciousness, and people everywhere begin 'to
perceive viable solutions to the maladies existing on Earth.
Lightworkers join together to create the perfection of
Heaven on Earth. As they do, all traces of pain and
suffering are transmuted into Light. Every concept of lack
and limitation ceases to exist, and the Abundance of God
floods the Earth. People perceive and acknowledge the
Divinity blazing in every Heart Flame.
Humanity now knows and accepts that all Life is Divine.
This realization inspires every person to feel and express
Love and mutual respect for every part of Life.*

*As the collective thoughts and feelings of Humanity
continually empower the perfection of Heaven on Earth,
the physical plane is transformed and transfigured.
The body of Mother Earth is restored to a verdant
Paradise of Splendor and Light.*

*The life of every living Being is filled with Love, Joy,
Happiness, Prosperity, Vibrant Health, Fulfillment,
Enlightenment, Eternal Peace, Harmony, Balance, Spiritual
Wisdom and every other Divine Quality of our
Father-Mother God.*

*Mother Earth dons her seamless garment of Light and
Ascends up the Spiral of Evolution into the full expression
of her new 5th-Dimensional Solar Reality.
The Heavens rejoice, and our Father-Mother God respond,*

*"Welcome HOME, Beloved Children. Well done."*

*And so it is. I AM, I AM, I AM.*

# CHAPTER TEN

# EXPANDING THE LIGHT OF OUR FATHER-MOTHER GOD ON EARTH

After the God-Victorious return of our Mother God, the balanced frequencies of our Father God's Power and our Mother God's Love, *the Violet Flame of God's Infinite Perfection*, expanded exponentially through every Heart Flame. This greatly enhanced Humanity's awakening, which triggered a global response.

For the next few years, awakening Lightworkers around the world joined with the Company of Heaven to cocreate literally thousands of activities of Light. Day by day, every Lightworker wove his or her unique gifts into the unfolding Divine Plan. The Golden Thread of each activity of Light was woven into Earth's Tapestry of Life, in preparation for the next step of our Ascension into the Light. Every Lightworker and every activity of Light were critical to the success of Earth's Ascension; none was more important than the other. Through these activities of Light, the patterns of perfection that would form the archetypes for the New Earth were created in the Realms of Cause.

Every physical manifestation begins with an archetype, a blueprint, that is created in the Realms of Cause by the thoughts and feelings of Humanity. The archetype is then magnetized into the world of effects, the physical plane, where it is empowered with the thoughts, words, feelings, and actions of people abiding in the physical plane. When enough of Humanity's energy is focused on the archetype, it is brought into form and tangibly manifests on Earth.

The moment when enough energy for physical manifestation is reached, is referred to in the science of Quantum Mechanics as a *"critical mass."* In modern-day parlance, this phenomenon is called *"the tipping point."* When something reaches critical mass, an unstoppable shift occurs and nothing can prevent the change from happening. The only variable is how long it will take Humanity to reach a critical mass for a particular archetype. It is important for us to understand this process, because it explains why sometimes our progress seems so slow. Knowing about reaching a critical mass will help us to see what we can do to more quickly manifest the changes we seek.

## REACHING CRITICAL MASS

A very common scenario is that when we begin to awaken, we become aware that our thoughts and feelings are creative faculties. This awareness prompts us to improve our behavior. We put forth the effort to think positively and to control our emotions. We focus our attention on what we want to manifest in our lives instead of focusing on our fears and the things that we do not like about our lives. We invoke the Light of God, and we empower our efforts with daily meditations, visualizations, and affirmations.

Often, after what seems like a valiant effort, we continue to experience some of the same old problems. This causes us to become discouraged and to lose trust in our ability to change our lives. At that point, we feel our efforts are futile, and we usually give up on trying to improve our situation. We stop invoking the Light, and we let go of our visions. This causes us to regress into our old, negative behavior patterns. We start dwelling on our fears, problems, and challenges. Instead of using our thoughts and feelings to empower our goals, our hopes, and our dreams, we amplify the very things we were striving to change. As a result of this relapse, things get worse, and our situation appears even more hopeless.

The laws of physics are responsible for this phenomenon. Once we understand how this physical plane works, we will muster up the courage to persevere, even in the face of apparent failure. We will be inspired to *"keep on keeping on,"* until we reach a critical mass and our goals are tangibly manifest in the physical plane.

Everything is comprised of energy, vibration and consciousness. When we explore a portion of the vast science of Quantum Mechanics, we learn that when something reaches critical mass, there is an *unstoppable shift* that takes place. For instance, when an electron is increasing in vibration, the moment it reaches a critical mass of the higher vibration, the entire electron is pulled up into the higher frequency and nothing can stop that shift.

Critical mass is determined by several factors and various conditions. To simplify our understanding, for our purposes here, the Beings of Light have asked us to think of critical mass as 51% of the energy, vibration and consciousness of whatever it is we are talking about. For instance, when 51% of an electron is vibrating at a higher frequency, it has reached a critical mass, and the remaining 49% is instantly absorbed into the new vibration. Once critical mass is reached, nothing can stop that shift. So, how does this facet of Quantum Mechanics affect our ability to transform our lives?

Let's talk about what happens when we invoke the balanced frequencies of our Father-Mother God—*the Violet Flame of God's Infinite Perfection*—to transmute the negativity manifesting in our lives. When we use the Violet Flame, the same laws of Quantum Mechanics apply. If we want to transmute poverty consciousness, for instance, we invoke the Violet Flame and ask that every electron of poverty consciousness we have ever expressed in any time frame or dimension be transmuted back into its Divine Potential, which is the Abundance of God. The moment 51% of our energy, vibration and consciousness from all time frames and dimensions is resonating with frequencies of God's Abundance instead of poverty, lack, and limitation, we will have reached a critical mass of prosperity consciousness. When that occurs, nothing can stop God's Abundance from manifesting in our lives.

The problem is that we never know just when we are going to reach that magical moment of critical mass. There are often no outer-world signs, and it may even look as if we are very far away from that instant of transformation. That is when we usually feel our efforts are failing, and we tend to give up. Sometimes we may be just a breath away from reaching critical mass, but we don't realize that, so we get discouraged and stop trying. Then we end up never reaching our goal.

The key to our success is that we must *"keep on keeping on,"* even in the face of adversity. It is vital for us to understand that the Violet Flame is infinitely more powerful than any fragmented human miscreation we may have deliberately or inadvertently created. Poverty has no power over the Abundance of God. Our Divine Potential is infinitely more powerful than disease, failure, dysfunctional relationships, hatred, greed, corruption, war, or any of the other humanly created maladies appearing on the screen of Life.

The only reason these things exist in our lives is because we forgot that we are cocreating this reality. We forgot that when we put our attention on these negative things, we empower them and sustain them in our lives. We forgot that we must continually focus on what we want to cocreate, not the things that we do not want.

It is important for us to comprehend that when we are talking about reaching a critical mass of energy, vibration, and consciousness, we are talking about every electron of precious Life energy we have ever released, in any time frame or dimension. This involves thousands of lifetimes. But remember, miracles have taken place. Just prior to Harmonic Concordance in November 2003, the most intensified cleansing the Earth and Humanity have ever experienced occurred. This was cocreated by the Company of Heaven and the I AM Presence of every man, woman, and child on the planet. Tons and tons of our human miscreations were purged and transmuted into Light. What was left for each of us to transmute is a mere fraction of our past misqualified energy.

Now we can choose to use the Violet Flame to transmute our remaining human miscreations, and consecrate our thoughts, words, feelings, and actions to empower only the positive experiences we want to create in our lives. If we do these two simple things, we will manifest our visions and dreams, and transform our lives into what we want them to be. This will occur sooner than we can fathom.

Even though it may have taken thousands of lifetimes for us to create the mess we are in, it will not take thousands of lifetimes to get us out of this mess. Light is infinitely more powerful than the fear-based, fragmented miscreations of our human egos. And do not forget, we have the entire Company of Heaven amplifying our efforts A THOUSAND TIMES A THOUSAND FOLD. This is why every prophecy has stated that in these "end times," the transformation will take place *"in the twinkling of an eye."* With this Divine Intervention, our success is assured.

This information is being reiterated by the Beings of Light during this critical moment to help us remember that if we do not like what is happening in our lives or in the world, we have the option, the ability, and the responsibility to do something about it. This is true for each of us individually, and it is true for all of us collectively as a global family.

# ANCHORING THE ARCHETYPES
# FOR THE NEW EARTH

After our initial ascent into the frequencies of the 5th Dimension, the Company of Heaven told Lightworkers that archetypes for the New Earth were forming in the Realms of Cause. This was occurring through the myriad activities of Light being conducted by people all over the world.

In 2008, these patterns of perfection reached a critical mass. This meant that the archetypes for the New Earth were ready to be anchored in the physical plane where they would be available for Humanity to empower, and to bring into tangible form. The Beings of Light said the most critical archetypes for the New Earth would be anchored first. These were the archetypes for *God's Abundance and Eternal Peace*. The Company of Heaven revealed that God's Abundance and Eternal Peace are inseparable aspects of our Father-Mother God. One of these Divine Qualities cannot exist without the other. Pulsating within the Golden Light of Eternal Peace is God's Abundance, and contained within the essence of God's Abundance are the frequencies of Eternal Peace.

Lightworkers were delighted when we realized that these were the first archetypes for the New Earth that would be anchored in the physical plane. This was what we had all been working toward. This was the Cosmic Moment when Humanity's descent into poverty consciousness would be reversed, and the archetypes for God's Abundance and Eternal Peace would be permanently established on Earth.

For some time, the Company of Heaven had been telling us that one of the greatest needs of the hour was for awakening Humanity to attain our financial freedom. This is a vital and necessary facet of the Divine Plan. The viable solutions for all of the maladies existing on Earth are beginning to flow from the Realms of Illumined Truth into the hearts and minds of Humanity. In order to bring these powerful solutions into physical manifestation, awakened people with a higher consciousness need to have the financial support to bypass the old paradigms of greed and corruption. It is the abuse of money and the compulsive greed of our human egos that have caused the appalling poverty and the inequitable distribution of wealth on this planet in the first place.

The Beings of Light have confirmed that at this very moment there are patterns of perfection in the Causal Body of God that contain practical solutions for every negative situation manifesting on Earth. This includes solutions to our energy crisis, pollution, global warming, disease, poverty, crime, aging, hunger, homelessness, war, and every other human miscreation. Amazingly, there are people who have been manipulated by their human egos into suppressing the knowledge and the technologies that are available to solve these problems. Through their limited, fear-based consciousness, all these people can see is what will happen to their present financial situations if these problems are solved.

For instance, what would happen if all of a sudden disease and the degenerative process of aging were eliminated from the planet? Imagine the number of people who would be out of work: doctors, nurses, hospitals, nursing homes, rehabilitation centers, pharmacies, drug companies, medical insurance companies, and all of the workers who support these industries. Millions of people have a vested interest in keeping us sick.

What would happen if war was eliminated? If you will remember, just before September 11, 2001, and the manifestation of the Afghanistan and Iraq wars, there was a lot of talk about having to close some of the military bases in the USA for financial reasons. This was causing a great deal of concern for military personnel. Look at the millions of people who would be out of work if our military complex and the war machine were no longer needed. There are millions of people who have a vested interest in perpetuating war.

What if Humanity remembers the Oneness of Life? What if we all recognize the Divinity within each other, and we truly develop a reverence for all Life? Crime, corruption, violence, greed, and everything associated with the criminal aspects of our present existence would be eliminated. Think of the number of people who would be out of work if we no longer needed the criminal justice system, police, security officers, prisons, prison guards, criminal lawyers, et cetera. What in the world would we watch on television or in the movies? It is interesting to observe that since many of the prisons in the USA have been privatized, the population of the prisons in this country has more than doubled. Prisons can not succeed as a private business without lots of prisoners. There are millions of people who are vested in keeping crime alive and well.

When we ask people if they want to see disease, war, and crime eliminated, they usually say *"of course."* But when their livelihoods depend on these things, they are afraid of what will happen to their financial security if these conditions cease to exist. That fear creates an underlying need that perpetuates the painful things people say they would like to eliminate.

We are so accustomed to living with disease, war, and crime that we think they are normal. We cannot even imagine living without them. The concept of a world without these maladies seems unrealistic and far too good to be true. Our Father-Mother God and the Company of Heaven are striving to remind us of the fact that these terrible things were never part of our Divine Plan. We created them through the misuse of our thoughts, words, feelings, and actions. It is time for us to stop this insanity. It is time to turn things around.

We must raise our consciousness. Instead of looking at the outer world and coming to the erroneous conclusion that this is all there is, we need to see the bigger picture. We are cocreating this reality. Everything existing on Earth at this time is the result of Humanity's collective consciousness. If we do not like what is happening in our individual lives or on the planet, we can join together and cocreate a new reality. All we have to do is have enough of us focusing our attention on the patterns of perfection for the New Earth to reach a critical mass.

When we lift up our consciousness, we realize that we can tap into the patterns of perfection in the Causal Body of God. We have the ability to cocreate wonderful new ventures and avenues of employment that will secure our financial freedom while blessing and enhancing all Life. We do not have to limit ourselves to the parameters of what currently exists on Earth. We do not have to perpetuate pain and suffering just so we will have enough money to survive. This distorted belief is a trap that our human egos created in order to control us.

The quandary we are in at this time is that we are Ascending into the 5th-Dimensional Realms of Light. This dimension vibrates with the frequencies of God's Infinite Perfection. Every frequency of vibration that is less than the harmony and balance of God cannot exist in the 5th Dimension. This is why all of the prophecies that describe the New Earth indicate that there will be no pain or suffering; no aging, disease, or death as we know it now; no poverty, hunger, or homelessness; no war or violence.

This miraculous transformation is not going to occur because Beloved Jesus rides in on a white cloud and magically does it all for us. It is going to occur, because you and I and every soul evolving on this planet remembers who we are and our purpose and reason for being. We are cocreators. It is time for us to reclaim our Divine Birthright, which is God's Infinite Abundance. This will allow us to let go of the belief that we have to perpetuate the maladies on Earth in order to have enough money for our survival.

Our challenge is that we have accepted for aeons of time the illusion that all of our human miscreations are normal. We actually expect the negativity existing on Earth to be part of our life experiences. We call the atrocities we inflict on each other *"human nature."* We carefully plan for all of the things that can go wrong in our lives. We even have a term called *"Murphy's Law."* This law states, *"If anything can go wrong, it will."* The intent of this belief system is to prepare us for the worst, then if anything better than that happens we can consider it a bonus. One person I know had such a jaded outlook on life that he said he thought Murphy was an optimist.

Those belief systems are being manipulated by our human egos. Our thoughts and feelings are creative. Whatever we focus our attention on through our thoughts, words, feelings, actions, and beliefs, we empower and sustain in our lives. When we expect and plan for things to go wrong, things go wrong. Do you know what you get when you save money for a rainy day? You get rainy days. It is important to save some of your money, but save for wonderful and life-enhancing things not catastrophes.

Plan and expect for things to go right. If something goes wrong, deal with it. But do not cocreate it with your plans and expectations. Empower what you want to happen with your thoughts and feelings, and transmute what you do not want to happen with the Violet Flame. When you reach a critical mass of positive expectations and plans, miracles will happen. You will be astonished at how smoothly things go in your life when you expect and plan for things to go right.

We are so used to dealing with pain and suffering that I have actually had people tell me that they cannot imagine anything more boring than living in harmony all of the time. That always amazes me, so I ask them to describe what they mean by harmony. In every case, I realize that the person is dealing with so much pain that whenever the pain stops for a moment he or she feels numb. Living without pain is so foreign it feels like there is something wrong. This feeling scares them, so they create a crisis. This new situation enables them to feel something again. Even though it is pain they are feeling, in his or her mind it is better to feel pain than to feel nothing at all.

When these people think of harmony, they remember the neutral zone where they did not feel anything. They do not have a pleasant memory of being without pain, so they think of harmony as being boring and not exciting. Well, being without pain is good, but that neutral zone is not harmony. It is just void of pain. Most of us have been so manipulated by our human egos that we have not even glimpsed real harmony.

In the higher frequencies of Light that we are moving into—the sacred space where our I AM Presences abide—the pulsations of Divine Harmony are glorious. They include the unfathomable Light of Divine Love, Peace, Happiness, Joy, Elation, Bliss, Ecstasy, Wonder, Awe, and every other Divine Quality of our Father-Mother God. I promise you, there is nothing boring about perpetually living in those ecstatic frequencies of harmony!

Usually when we think of these blissful gifts of Light, we assume that they will be available only when *"we die and go to Heaven,"* but that is wrong. They are available to each and every one of us right here and right now. These are the archetypes for the New Earth. These are the patterns of perfection that we have cocreated in the Realms of Cause and will now tangibly manifest in the physical plane. The time for us to do that is NOW!

In August 2008 during the 21st anniversary of Harmonic Convergence, Lightworkers from all over the world gathered within the forcefield of Archangel Michael's Temple of Power and Protection. This focus of Light pulsates in, through, and around the pristine beauty of Lake Louise, and the exquisite mountains near Banff in Alberta, Canada.

The Lightworkers gathered at Lake Louise were joined in consciousness by hundreds of thousands of Lightworkers who were tuning in from locations all over the planet. Together, we served as surrogates on behalf of ALL Humanity. The Lightworkers formed a mighty transformer of Light through which the archetypes for the New Earth were anchored in the physical world of form. These patterns of perfection included the archetypes for God's Abundance and Eternal Peace.

After the archetypes were anchored on Earth, the Company of Heaven joined with the I AM Presence of every person and created the sacred space to purge the thoughts and feelings of Humanity that were reflecting poverty consciousness. This cleansing process was a critical step in paving the way for the physical manifestation of the archetypes for God's Abundance and Eternal Peace.

The Legions of Light revealed that the year 2008 was recorded in the annals of history as the Cosmic Moment when Humanity reclaimed our Divine Birthright of God's Abundance. Our descent into poverty consciousness was reversed, and the NEW archetypes for God's Infinite Abundance and Eternal Peace were permanently anchored on this planet.

As the archetypes for God's Abundance and Eternal Peace expanded through the physical, etheric, mental, and emotional strata of Earth, everything that conflicted with those patterns of perfection was pushed to the surface to be transmuted into Light.

The core of purity was activated in every electron of precious Life energy that was reflecting the human miscreations of greed, corruption, selfishness, poverty, lack, limitation, and the abuse of power. This caused the cloak of darkness that was encapsulating these electrons to be cast off and pushed to the surface of Humanity's conscious minds and experiences. This purging allowed these deplorable human miscreations to be exposed in the Light of God.

By the middle of September 2008, Humanity began experiencing the shocking results of this appalling greed and unconscionable corruption. Wall Street and the world banking systems had brought the global economy to the brink of total collapse. People everywhere were living beyond their means; many of them had indebted themselves far beyond their capacity to pay for their mortgages or their bills. Countries all over the world were on the verge of a catastrophic depression. Once again, we were shown the lengths our fear-based human egos will go to gratify their compulsive and obsessive addictions.

It is important for us to know that our Father-Mother God would not have allowed this cleansing to take place with such intensity if it was going to cause more harm than good. It was allowed at this unprecedented level, so that we will quickly move through the negativity and begin to tangibly experience God's Abundance and Eternal Peace on a global scale. In the midst of this intensified purging process, the archetypes for God's Abundance and Eternal Peace are being expanded moment by moment by Lightworkers around the world. The Violet Flame is being invoked daily and hourly to transmute the surfacing human miscreations as fast as possible.

The greed, corruption, selfishness, and abuse of power we are witnessing cannot and will not exist on the 5th-Dimensional

New Earth. Any financial system or institution that is based in greed or any other corrupt or fraudulent practice is going to be turned upside down. These institutions are doomed to failure. Individuals whose human egos are committed to greed, corruption, and fraud will also experience the full brunt of their selfish activities. There are people who are fighting tooth and nail to regain their power and to hold on to their malevolent schemes, but they will not ultimately succeed. This purification process will wreak havoc in their lives. The old paradigms of greed and corruption are now obsolete. Regardless of the illusion of outer appearances, the Law of the Circle is scientific and accurate to the letter.

It is vital for people to know that it is not the Divine Intent of our Father-Mother God for this cleansing process to take awakening Humanity down the tubes financially. On the contrary, we have been given incredible tools to assist us with transmuting poverty consciousness. These tools are sacred gifts, specifically designed to help each of us release the past and establish new patterns of prosperity consciousness, which will quickly open us to the flow of God's Abundance and Eternal Peace This sacred knowledge is flowing through every open door. It is readily available to anyone who is willing to lift up in consciousness and to accept his or her reality as a Beloved Child of God.

The first thing we need to do in order to reclaim our Divine Birthright of God's Abundance and Eternal Peace, is clear our relationship with money. There is so much confusion and fear about money that even though we think we desperately need it, we are blocking its natural flow in our lives. Let's join together and transcend this problem.

# CHAPTER ELEVEN

# CLEARING OUR RELATIONSHIP WITH MONEY

For aeons of time, our human egos have manipulated us through poverty consciousness. This is the basis of all of our problems relating to money. Sometimes poverty consciousness caused us to become obsessed with money, which resulted in greed and the compulsion to acquire and hoard wealth through any means and at any cost. At other times, it caused us to believe that there is not enough money for us to live comfortably, which resulted in manifesting the dire conditions of hunger, homelessness, and every other extreme lack or limitation in life. I am sure we have all experienced both extremes and everything in between many times throughout our Earthly sojourns.

In an attempt to stop our egos' obsession with money, the world religions developed beliefs and rules to prevent money from being such an issue in our lives. In some cases, we were told that in order to be a good person we must reject money. We were given the impression that somehow poverty is a virtue. Some religious disciplines even require that we take vows of poverty. There are statements in the Bible and in other religious teachings that have been interpreted with the deliberate intent of proving to us that money is evil, and that only bad people acquire wealth.

One statement we often hear from the pulpit is, *"The Bible says, 'money is the root of all evil'."* That is not what the Bible says at all. The Bible says, *"The WORSHIP of money is the root of all evil,"* which is a very different concept. All we have to do is observe what is going on in the global economy to confirm that, indeed, people who worship money are wreaking havoc in the world. Another statement we often hear is, *"A camel can pass through the eye of a needle more easily than a rich man can get into Heaven."* Well, of course a camel cannot pass through the eye of a needle, so that must mean that a rich man cannot get into Heaven. Right? Actually, that is not right.

Jesus said that when he gave his teachings, he used examples that the people he was speaking to could understand. This is true for all of the teachers who preceded him as well. When Jesus' teachings were translated, often centuries after he gave them, the scribes did not understand some of the examples he and the other teachers used. To compensate for their lack of understanding, the scribes tried to literally interpret what they were reading or being told through oral traditions. Consequently, many of the statements in the Bible that are now being taught as literal facts have been misinterpreted. The statement, *"A camel can pass through the eye of a needle more easily than a rich man can get into Heaven,"* is usually interpreted inaccurately.

Jesus said that 2,000 years ago, there was a wall around Jerusalem to protect people from the criminal elements outside of the city. The ruins of that wall exist to this day. There was a small opening in the wall through which the traders passed in and out of Jerusalem. The opening in the wall was called *"the eye of the needle."*

In the mornings, the traders and their camels would squeeze through the small opening on their way to market. At night, they would return to the wall after they had purchased all of the items they wanted to bring back to Jerusalem to sell. The camels could not fit through the opening with all of the worldly goods on their backs, so they had to remove their wares in order to pass through the *"eye of the needle."* What Jesus meant by his statement is not that a rich man cannot get into Heaven, but that we cannot take our worldly possessions with us when we leave this physical plane.

The problem we are having now is that we are awakening,

and we are beginning to remember who we are and why we are on Earth at this time. With this awareness, we realize that God's Abundance is our Divine Birthright, and that God's supply of all good things is infinite. So we ask ourselves, *"If this is true, why are we in the financial mess we are in?"* The answer is simple. The reason we continue to experience poverty is because we are always the sum total of everything we have ever cocreated. As long as the majority of energy associated with our thoughts, words, feelings, and actions from all time frames and dimensions is vibrating with poverty consciousness, we are going to have financial challenges. The moment we reach a critical mass of prosperity consciousness, everything will shift, and God's Abundance will become our natural state of Being. This is what our Father-Mother God intended for us in the first place.

In our various lifetimes, we have experienced the gamut of conditions and circumstances involving money. We have at one time or another rejected money by taking vows of poverty. We have also felt the incredible pain of not having enough money to sustain our physical bodies comfortably. At the other end of the spectrum, there have been times when we accumulated great wealth and used it selfishly to manipulate and control people. Abusing money has been the order of the day on this planet for a very long time.

As a result of our past behavior, we all have etheric records and memories that subconsciously tell us money is bad, and it causes pain. We also have etheric memories that tell us we will abuse money if we have too much of it, and that we cannot be spiritual if we are wealthy. So in order for us to clear our relationship with money, this is where we need to begin. We need to reprogram our thinking about money, and we need to transmute our obsolete patterns of poverty consciousness through all time frames and dimensions back to the *"Fall."*

First and foremost, we must accept that *poverty is not a virtue*. Poverty is demeaning and humiliating. It is painful and causes all manner of suffering. It causes family problems, health problems, mental problems, and emotional problems. We are not more spiritual or better people if we are poor.

We can do much more good and help many more people if we have money than if we do not have money. Poverty prevents us from being free to fulfill our Divine Plans. It is a sign that we are not fulfilling our covenant with our Father-Mother God. We have accepted our gift of Life, but over our many lifetimes we have not balanced that gift by adding to the Light of the world as we promised. We know this is true, because we would be financially free if the Light we have added to the world balanced the Lifeforce we have received from our Father-Mother God. This is a profound Truth. It is the fulfillment of the Law of the Circle, which we are all subject to on this planet. We need to rectify this imbalance. If we are going to attain our financial freedom, we have no other option.

## RECLAIMING GOD'S ABUNDANCE

I would like to very briefly reiterate what the Beings of Light have shared with us regarding our covenant with our Father-Mother God, and what we must now do to fulfill our end of the bargain and to reclaim God's Abundance.

In the beginning, our Father-Mother God and the Elemental Kingdom agreed to provide us with everything we would need to comfortably sustain our physical bodies during our Earthly sojourns. We were given the radiance of the Sun, fresh air, water, food, and materials from which to build shelters and make clothing for ourselves. Our God Parents provided us with our Lifeforce, the electronic Light substance that beats our hearts and allows us to live, move, breathe, think, and feel in the physical plane. The Divine Intent was for our physical needs to be taken care of, so that we could focus on using our gift of free will and our creative faculties of thought and feeling to learn to be cocreators with our Father-Mother God.

It was never the Divine Plan that we struggle from morning until night in mundane jobs just to put food on the table and a roof over our heads. That, in fact, is a gross distortion of the original Divine Plan for this planet, and it is a cumbersome distraction from our purpose and reason for being in this school of learning.

After the "Fall," we lost awareness of our Divine Heritage. We forgot that we are Children of God, and that all our Father-Mother God have is ours. As we descended into denser and denser frequencies, we were unable to hear the guidance of our Christ Selves. To compensate for that void in our lives, we developed our fragmented, fear-based human egos. We gave our power away to this mutated aspect of ourselves and allowed it to manipulate us into believing that all we are is our physical bodies and that the physical plane is all that exists.

With that distorted perception, we started believing in lack and limitation. We forgot that we are cocreating this reality and that the unformed primal Light that comprises every particle of Life in the physical plane is limitless. We forgot about God's Infinite Abundance, and we started fearing for our very lives. We became afraid that there was not going to be enough of the necessities of life in order for everyone to survive on this planet.

This caused us to hoard the things we needed to sustain our physical bodies which, in turn, blocked the flow of God's Abundance. We are cocreators with our Father-Mother God, so when our fear-based thoughts and feelings reflected on the elemental substance of the Earth, we started experiencing inclement weather conditions which resulted in floods, droughts, famines, plagues, and pestilence. When that happened, we were catapulted into a vicious circle. The more we hoarded the things we needed to survive, the less the necessities of life were made available to us, and the more afraid we became.

We developed a consciousness of greed and selfishness, which we believed was necessary in order to survive. We started fighting with each other over land, food, water, and material things. Eventually we created a monetary system to barter for the very things God had freely given to each of us. As the confusion and chaos built in momentum, our human egos coerced us into believing that whatever we needed to do to survive was appropriate, even if it meant lying, stealing, cheating, or killing.

As we witness the meltdown within the global economy, we can clearly see the evidence of this tragic situation everywhere we look. Practically every malady manifesting on Earth can be traced back to the fear-based consciousness of lack and limitation. That is true whether we are talking about the corruption and moral depravity associated with governments; the military; financial institutions; corporations; the medical, insurance, and pharmaceutical industries; religious organizations; educational institutions; profit and nonprofit organizations; or individuals in the private sector.

Our ego-based fear for survival infuses Humanity with a willingness to do whatever it takes to get what we want. For aeons of time, people have continually acted out of the distorted perception of lack and limitation. As a result of that illusion, people everywhere are writhing in the pain and suffering our human egos perpetuated by entrapping us in poverty consciousness.

It is time for us to take back the power our human egos have usurped from us, and it is time for us to give our I AM Presence full dominion of our lives. We have the ability to reclaim our Divine Heritage and to restore the limitless flow of God's Abundance. Never has it been more important for us to do so.

As the archetypes for God's Abundance and Eternal Peace expand on the New Earth, and the negativity that conflicts with that Light is pushed to the surface to be transmuted and healed, we are seeing the global economy reel on the shifting sands of corruption and greed. From outer appearances, it looks like the economy is headed for total collapse, but, in fact, *this is the darkness before the dawn.*

The purging that is taking place in the economic world is a necessary part of the healing process. The old-age archetypes of greed, selfishness, corruption, and moral depravity are being exposed and shattered in order to clear the way for the new archetypes of God's Abundance and Eternal Peace. Those who are willing to attain their wealth by harming another part of Life are doomed to failure. Whether they are hurting people or polluting the Earth, their nefarious efforts are being exposed in the radiant Light of Divine Truth.

The dog-eat-dog, looking-out-for-number-one selfishness that has been so prevalent over the years cannot be sustained now that the new archetypes are in place. This is the time that has been prophesied when *"All that is hidden must now be revealed."* The clandestine schemes of deception and dishonesty that have trapped the multitudes in a web of poverty and fear will not be concealed in a cloak of darkness any longer. The elite few who hoard the wealth of the world while millions live in hunger, disease, and squalor will no longer succeed in their self-obsessed ventures.

Poverty is a human miscreation, and it was never intended to be part of our Divine Plan. The distorted patterns of lack and limitation are an illusion that we created, and that we are sustaining through our thoughts, words, feelings, actions, and beliefs.

The new archetypes of God's Abundance and Eternal Peace are based on the Divine Truth that *God is our supply*, not outer world circumstances. Our natural heritage is God's continual supply of all good things. When we remember this Truth, we open our hearts once again to the infinite flow of God's Abundance.

This unique moment will be recorded in the Golden Book of Life as the time in which the Era of Eternal Peace and Infinite Abundance was permanently established on Earth. Just imagine, you and I are physically present to cocreate the events that will lift this planet and all her Life into the Light of Eternal Peace and God's Infinite Abundance.

In order for us to reclaim our natural Birthright of God's Infinite Abundance, we need to clear our relationship with money. Since we have chosen to live in a system that uses money as our source of exchange, we need to eliminate our fear of it and realize that money is just a source of energy—*period*. It is not some awesome entity that comes into our lives to wield its power over us and rule our destinies. It is only because of our fear for survival that we have allowed money to have that kind of control over us.

First of all, we must eliminate poverty consciousness and start functioning with prosperity consciousness. Instead of worrying all of the time about not having enough money, we need to focus on gratitude for the money we do have. Gratitude is a magnet that brings more of what we are grateful for into our lives.

Every time we spend a penny of our money, whether it is to buy groceries, pay our bills, provide entertainment, or whatever, we should bless it with gratitude for the service it is providing to us. Then we should let it go freely, *knowing* that money is just *a source of energy* and, like ALL energy, it will go out, expand and return to us for more service.

If we send our money forth grudgingly, bemoaning the high cost of living, fearing we won't have enough to cover our expenses, hating to spend it on the necessities of life, we will automatically block the flow of God's Abundance.

The process of developing prosperity consciousness does not mean going out and charging unnecessary things and getting ourselves deeper in debt by spending money we do not have. It does mean, however, that we recognize money is providing a service to us that we should accept with gratitude and appreciation.

As we move forward at warp speed, it is crucial for us to remember that we are responsible for cocreating our own prosperity. We must perpetually ask ourselves, *"Is what I AM thinking, saying, feeling, or doing adding to my prosperity and prosperity consciousness, or am I blocking my prosperity with fear and poverty consciousness?"*

If what we are expressing is reflecting poverty consciousness, then we must ask ourselves, *"What do I need to change in order to express prosperity consciousness and open to God's Abundance right now?"* It is imperative that we hold tenaciously to our positive visions and energize them daily with our affirmations and the focus of our attention. We must be deliberate about our wealth. Through persistence, confidence, and acceptance, we will open our hearts to God's supply of all good things.

# A VITAL FACTOR IN RECEIVING
# GOD'S ABUNDANCE

The Law of the Circle plays a very important role in our prosperity. The ebb and flow of Life, which is so clearly demonstrated in the Law of the Circle, is a critical factor in order for us to receive the flow of God's Infinite Abundance. There are many expressions that describe the ebb and flow of our Lifeforce: inbreath and outbreath, radiation and magnetization, giving and receiving, cause and effect, action and reaction, involution and evolution. In order for the Divine Plan to be fulfilled and for us to receive a continual flow of God's Abundance, the ebb and flow of our gift of Life must be *balanced*. If we are receiving more Lifeforce than we are sending out or vice versa, an imbalance is created that blocks the flow.

When we volunteered to embody on Earth to learn how to become cocreators with our Father-Mother God, we agreed that we would cooperate with the Universal Law of the Circle and maintain the balance of our Lifeforce. Our Father-Mother God agreed to provide our Lifeforce and everything we would need to sustain our bodies, and, in return, we agreed that we would balance our gift of Life by using our Lifeforce to add to the Light of the world. This is easily done through expressions of love, reverence for all Life, gratitude, wisdom, abundance, peace, joy, happiness, and everything else that blesses all Life on Earth.

When we fell into the abyss of our own human miscreations, we forgot about the agreements we made with God. Even though we were still receiving and using all of the gifts of Life our Father-Mother God were providing for us, we were not giving anything back in return. We were not fulfilling our part of the agreement by balancing the gifts of Life we were utilizing. We were not using our Lifeforce to add to the Light of the world. That self-centered behavior effectively blocked the flow of God's Abundance.

Once our supply was blocked, we fell into the dysfunctional pattern of struggling every day just to make enough money to pay for the things we needed to sustain our physical bodies. Those were the same things that God had already given to us for free. When we expend our time, energy, and money to pay for what God has already provided for us, it is like not giving anything back at all to balance our gift of Life. That imbalance trapped us in a mode of stagnation. As a result, we were cast into the paralyzing throes of poverty which only perpetuated our consciousness of lack and limitation.

That perplexing condition is the cause of the poverty we have experienced over many lifetimes, and it is the reason for the financial situations that are affecting the global economy. The good news is that we created this problem, and we have the power to do something about it. *We have the ability to renew our covenant with God and to reclaim our prosperity.*

All we have to do to renew our covenant with God is to begin doing what we agreed to do in the first place. That means that we need to balance the gift of Life we receive and benefit from every day by giving something back in return that adds to the Light of the world. That may sound complicated, but it is actually very simple. *Anything* we do to improve the quality of Life on Earth adds to the Light of the world. Whatever we do to bless Life in the way of sharing our love, reverence, adoration, gratitude, wisdom, abundance, peace, joy, and happiness further enhances the manifestation of the archetypes for the New Earth and adds to the Light of the world.

There are as many ways to open to the flow of God's Abundance as there are people on the planet. But if we specifically want to increase the abundance of *money* in our lives, there is a very specific process we must follow.

## INCREASING OUR CASH FLOW

At the present time, we use money as our means of exchange, so in order for us to attain prosperity and to become financially free, we need to increase our flow of money. We can easily do that by applying the Universal Law of the Circle. Remember, like attracts like. What we send out in the form of energy expands and returns to us. Money is energy. In order for us to attract more money into our lives, we need to send out more *money*.

Needless to say, we are all sending out lots of money to pay for our bodily needs. The problem is, God already provided those things to us for free. So the money we spend for our bodily needs does not count as the energy we must give back to God to balance the gift of our Lifeforce. In order to balance our Lifeforce and increase our cash flow, we must give some money back to God that is over and above what we spend to sustain our physical bodies.

The *spiritual key* to increasing our cash flow is for us to give a portion of our money away to people or organizations that will use it to improve the quality of Life on this planet. In other words, add to the Light of the world. There are myriad ways we can accomplish this. We can give money to institutions, organizations, charities, spiritual groups, religious groups, peace groups, corporations, human- or animal-rights groups, environmental groups, human endeavors associated with science, medicine, research, alternative fuel, the arts, education, sustainable development, or to any other person, place, condition or thing that we know is working to improve life on this planet with reverence and a genuine desire to cocreate the wonders of the New Earth.

The general consensus is that if we give as little as *ten percent* of our income back to God in appreciation for our gift of Life, we will reclaim the influx of God's Abundance. Then we will have all of the money we need to live in comfort and to joyously fulfill our Divine Plans.

. The attitude and consciousness with which we give our money away is critical to our success. Our money must be freely given away with no strings attached. We cannot expect anything in return from the people or places we give our donations to other than for them to use the money for the highest good of all concerned and to improve the quality of life on the planet.

We do not expect anything in return from the people or places we give our money to, *but we do expect that our donation is going to bless all Life, and that God's Abundance will expand our money tenfold on its return to us.* Once we give our money away, it is important for us to acknowledge and accept that, in compliance with the Law of the Circle, the money will expand and return to us bringing the God supply of all good things.

The reason we need to consciously affirm the return of our money is because we have forgotten that money is a form of energy, which should have been going out, expanding, and returning to us all along. We have just been blocking that natural process with our poverty consciousness.

Through the distorted perception of our human egos, we have developed the expectation that money goes out, but that it never comes back. By affirming our Divine Birthright and decreeing to accept God's Abundance, we reprogram ourselves to expect prosperity. We can start by claiming a tenfold return of our gift, but in Truth, there is no limit to the return we can expect. When we state the following decree with deep feeling, we affirm our gift of love and appreciation and claim God's Abundance on the return current. With every donation you give, affirm with deep feeling:

*With this donation, I AM giving __($100.00)__ back to God in love and appreciation for my gift of Life.*

*With the highest good of all concerned, I AM gratefully receiving __($1000.00)__ from the flow of God's Abundance on the return current.*

Once we give our love and appreciation for our gift of Life back to God in the energy of money and claim a tenfold return from God's Abundance, it is important for us to *consciously expect* to receive an increase of money. We must not limit God by trying to figure out where the money will come from; we just need to be open and receptive to every single avenue of return.

Each time we receive unexpected money or someone buys something for us or pays for something that we thought we were going to have to pay for ourselves, we should accept that this is God's Abundance flowing back into our lives. If things we need are on sale or if our bills are less than we thought they were going to be, that is our gift of money coming back to us. If someone gives us an item that we thought we were going to have to purchase or we get a raise or a higher-paying job, we are receiving God's Abundance. If someone finally pays an old debt that we thought was lost forever or we receive a bigger refund than we were expecting on our income tax return, we should acknowledge the money is part of our returning abundance.

When we participate in giving and receiving our money in love and appreciation for our gift of Life, God's Abundance becomes an ever-present state of Being in our lives. The more we fulfill our original agreement with God, by balancing our gift of Life and adding to the Light of the world through our thoughts, words, feelings, actions, and money, the sooner we will be financially free.

# TRANSMUTING POVERTY CONSCIOUSNESS

The following invocations and visualizations are gifts that have been given to Humanity by the Beings of Light in the Realms of Illumined Truth. The Divine Intent of these celestial sharings is to help all of us quickly manifest abundance and transmute the poverty consciousness we have cocreated over aeons of time. When we join together and invoke these activities of Light on a regular basis, we accelerate the process of reaching a critical mass. Then we will manifest God's Abundance and Eternal Peace tangibly in our lives.

All is in readiness. To participate in these activities of Light, please sit comfortably in your chair with your arms and legs uncrossed, your spine as straight as possible. Rest your hands gently in your lap with your palms facing upward.

Breathe in deeply, and as you exhale, let all of the tension of the day just drop away. Feel yourself becoming completely relaxed. Breathe in deeply again, and as you exhale, feel your I AM Presence take full dominion of your physical, etheric, mental, and emotional bodies. Your mind is activated. Any confusion, doubt, or fear are just swept away. You are mentally alert and vibrantly aware. You realize that, through the radiance of your I AM Presence, you are enveloped in a forcefield of invincible protection. This powerful forcefield of Light prevents anything from distracting you or interfering with this sacred activity of Light.

Feel the warmth of inner peace and well-being expanding through your Heart Flame. This is a gift from your I AM Presence.

Experience the buoyant joy of expectancy and enthusiasm. Accept and know that you are now an open door that no one can shut.

Now please follow me through this visualization with the full power of your attention. I am writing in the first person, so each of you will experience this activity of Light tangibly and personally in your own life. But know that you are simultaneously serving as a surrogate on behalf of all Humanity. Through the sacred space that you are holding now, the I AM Presence of every man, woman, and child is able to participate in this activity of Light in perfect alignment with each one's highest good and Divine Plan.

I AM my I AM Presence. My physical, etheric, mental, and emotional bodies are being raised in vibration. My awareness is increasing, and I hear the *"still, small voice within me."* As I lift up in consciousness, I experience new and exquisite vibrations. My entire Being is flooded with this resplendent Light. From this new level of awareness, I know, as never before,

*I AM my I AM Presence.*
*I AM a Being of radiant Light.*
*I AM One with the energy and vibration that is the*
*all-encompassing Presence of my Father-Mother God.*
*I AM One with the Divine Love that fills the Universe*
*with the glory of itself.*
*I AM One with every particle of Life.*
*I AM One with the Divine Plan for Planet Earth.*
*I AM One with the infinite flow of God's Abundance.*
*I AM that I AM.*

A reactivation and initiation into multidimensional awareness is now occurring within me. I AM being raised in vibration into the very Heart of God. The pre-encoded memories that were implanted deep within my cellular patterns aeons ago are being activated.

These patterns reveal my Divine Plan, my purpose and reason for Being. I experience a great soaring and awakening as I remember my Divine Heritage; I AM a Beloved Child of God.

I now step through the doorway into multidimensional realms of Light. Here I AM empowered with even more rarified frequencies of my Father-Mother God's Light. Moment-by-moment, this radiant Light is awakening within me previously untapped levels of wisdom and illumination. I easily grasp each new thought and idea as it enters my consciousness. Avenues of opportunity are unfolding before me. I feel a sense of elation as each opportunity presents itself. I joyously accept these Divine Opportunities, and I feel a greater sense of self-worth and accomplishment than ever before. My life is pulsating with a new sense of meaning and purpose.

I AM now lifted higher into the Realms of Perfection— and now higher—and now higher.  In this realm, I easily release and let go of attachments and behavior patterns that do not support my highest good. I release all patterns that reflect a consciousness less than prosperity and God's Infinite Abundance. I realize *this is the moment of my new beginning.*

I now have the ability to create prosperity consciousness for myself, and I do so easily and joyously.

*I AM experiencing my true integrity.*
*I AM trustworthy and honest.*
*I AM an expression of Divine Truth.*
*I AM worthy and deserving of prosperity, and*
*I AM able to transform every aspect of my life now.*

Change is manifesting in my life through God's Divine Grace and Love. Every aspect of my life that needs changing now surfaces before me. I observe these things objectively, and I let them go, one by one. I blaze the Violet Flame through the things that need changing in my life, and I love them free. I forgive myself for all of my perceived transgressions.

I know I AM a Child of God, and I deserve to be loved and forgiven. As the changes take place within me, I experience inner calm, patience, and silence.

I AM my I AM Presence. I AM One with the infinite intelligence within me, and I AM able to perceive viable solutions and make positive choices in all aspects of my life. I love myself unconditionally, and I AM grateful for this opportunity to change, which I accept with deep humility.

The Divine Power to sustain these changes is continually flowing through me, and from this moment forth, I choose to create a life of prosperity and do only that which supports my highest good.

Once again I AM lifted higher into the Realms of Perfection—and now higher—and now higher. I now focus on my Holy Breath. I realize that with every *inbreath* I extend in consciousness into Infinity, to the Source of never-ending perfection. With every *outbreath,* I magnetize the full momentum of that perfection and radiate its full blessing to all Life evolving on Earth.

My inbreath is the portal into the Pure Land of Boundless Splendor and Infinite Light, and my outbreath is the open door for all Divine Blessings for Humanity and the planet. I understand now that the Divine Gifts being presented to Humanity from the Legions of Light serving this sweet Earth will be drawn into the world of form on the Holy Breath.

I consecrate and dedicate myself to be the open door for these sacred gifts of Light.

*Father-Mother God, make me an instrument*
*for your Infinite Abundance.*

I AM now ready to release, let go of, and transmute every frequency of vibration and every single electron of precious Life energy I have ever released in any time frame or dimension that is expressing a pattern less than God's Abundance.

I AM enveloped in an invincible forcefield of protection and Eternal Peace. I AM able to review my life as an objective observer. I ask my I AM Presence to push to the surface of my conscious mind every experience I have ever had, both known and unknown, that is in any way preventing me from attaining prosperity.

As these experiences begin to surface, I invoke the Violet Flame from the Heart of my Father-Mother God. I absorb the most powerful frequencies of the Violet Flame that I AM capable of receiving. I breathe this Sacred Fire in, through, and around all of the energy that is surfacing and returning to me now to be loved free. The Violet Flame instantly transmutes the negative thoughts, words, actions, feelings, beliefs, and memories that are blocking my eternal financial freedom. Every electron of energy is being transformed back into its original perfection.

My I AM Presence now expands this activity of Light and reaches back through the Ages of time to magnetize every electron of energy stamped with my individual electronic pattern into the gift of the Violet Flame. These records and memories surface effortlessly, and I AM able to let them go without pain or fear. I feel the buoyant joy of freedom.

I continue breathing in as I reach deeper into the Violet Flame. As I exhale, the Violet Flame floods the physical plane of Earth. I affirm with deep feeling and a true inner knowing:

*I AM a force of the Violet Flame, greater than anything less than prosperity.*

I now realize I AM able to transmute, through the power of the Violet Flame, the mass consciousness of poverty. All records and memories of Humanity's abuse of the substance of money now flow into the Violet Flame.

Under the direction of my I AM Presence and the entire Company of Heaven, every electron of poverty consciousness that has ever been released by any part of Life, in any time frame or dimension, both known and unknown, is surfacing to be transmuted back into Light.

Transmutation is taking place as each electron enters the Violet Flame. Every trace of poverty consciousness is instantly transmuted—cause, core, effect, record, and memory—back into the frequencies of prosperity and God's Abundance.

*I AM a force of the Violet Flame,*
*greater than anything less than prosperity.*

*I AM a force of the Violet Flame,*
*greater than anything less than prosperity.*

*I AM a force of the Violet Flame,*
*greater than anything less than prosperity.*

*I AM Free! I AM Free! I AM Free!*
*I AM Eternally Financially Free!*

Beloved Father-Mother God, I ask through the Presence of God pulsating in my heart, that this activity of Light be maintained and eternally self-sustained. I ask that it be increased daily and hourly with every breath I take, until I reach a critical mass of prosperity consciousness, and God's Infinite Abundance is a manifest reality in my life.    And so it is.

## ABUNDANCE IS THE PATH TO PEACE

Through the Divinity pulsating in my heart, I consecrate my life now to the reestablishment of my covenant with God. I clearly know and understand with my new level of Divine Consciousness, that whatever I AM thinking, feeling, saying, or doing I AM empowering, cocreating, and magnetizing into my life.

From this moment forth, I dedicate my thoughts, words, actions, and feelings to empowering and cocreating the patterns of perfection for the New Earth. I begin with me, but I know that simultaneously I AM a surrogate serving on behalf of all Humanity, for we are all One. As I AM lifted up, all Life is lifted up with me.

I invoke the entire Company of Heaven and the I AM Presence of every man, woman, and child to come forth now. Blessed Ones, please assist me in this holy endeavor, and empower these activities of Light a thousand times a thousandfold.

## I AM COCREATING THE NEW EARTH

*I remember who I AM, and I love and respect myself as a*
*Beloved Child of God.*

*I AM enveloped in the invincible protection of*
*God's glorious Light and Divine Love*
*as I sojourn through my Earthly experiences.*

*I AM manifesting limitless physical perfection in my
physical, etheric, mental, and emotional bodies.
I AM vibrantly healthy and eternally youthful.
I AM filled with Divine Love, and I AM cocreating
wonderful, loving relationships in every avenue of my life.*

*I AM continually receiving the infinite flow of
God's Abundance, and I AM financially FREE.*

*I AM fulfilling my Divine Purpose,
and I AM financially and creatively rewarded in my job.*

*I AM an exponent and example of Divine Family Life,
including my place in the family of Humanity.*

*I AM reaching my Divine Potential as a Child of God in all
of my experiences as a son or daughter, a wife or husband,
a mother or father, a grandmother or grandfather,
a woman or man, as a friend, a relative, a co-worker,
a steward of the Earth, a teacher, a way shower,
a Lightworker, and a cocreator of Heaven on Earth.*

*I AM an Open Door for the Infinite Light
of God's Eternal Peace and Abundance.*

*I AM a living example of Divine Love, Trust, Integrity,
Honesty, Tolerance, and Reverence for ALL Life.*

*I AM able to listen, understand, and communicate openly
and honestly with every person on Earth.*

*I AM effortlessly Ascending into the
Divine Heart and Mind of God with every
Holy Breath I take.*

*I AM tapping into the Divine Guidance and the viable
solutions that will assist me in fulfilling my Divine Plan.
I AM an empowered Instrument of God.*

*I AM open to the Divine Guidance of my I AM Presence
and the Legions of Light in the Realms of Illumined Truth.
I easily communicate with these Beings of Light through
open-heart and open-mind telepathic communication.*

*I AM One with ALL Life, and I communicate openly with
the Angelic and Elemental Kingdoms as well.*

*I AM fulfilling my Divine Plan
and the Divine Plan for Beloved Mother Earth.*

*I AM cocreating the New Earth
with every thought, word, action, and feeling I express.*

*And so it is. I AM that I AM.*

## ETERNAL PEACE AND GOD'S ABUNDANCE

The Golden Rays of Eternal Peace and Abundance from the Causal Body of God are now flowing through the cup of my consciousness into the heart of every person on Earth. This Golden Light is pulsating with frequencies of the 5th Dimension beyond anything Humanity has ever experienced. Contained within the essence of the Flame of Eternal Peace is God's Abundance, and contained within the essence of God's Abundance is the Flame of Eternal Peace.

I breathe in deeply, and I become One with this Golden Light as I enter the secret place of the Most High Living God within my heart. As I enter this sacred space on the Holy Breath, I AM open and receptive to the impulses pouring forth from the

Heart and Mind of God. The hour has at last arrived, and the Divine Fiat has been issued by my Father-Mother God for the Divinity pulsating within my Heart Flame to be given full liberty and freedom of expression. My I AM Presence rejoices in this Divine Edict and will now give me every possible assistance in manifesting the patterns of perfection for the New Earth.

I AM a Keeper of the Flame of Eternal Peace and Abundance in accordance with my Divine Destiny. My Earthly bodies are perfectly balanced, and the latent powers encoded within my Heart Flame are activated. The abilities I developed over aeons of time that will assist me in cocreating the New Earth are brought into a balanced state of true mastery within me.

The Immortal Victorious Threefold Flame within my heart begins to expand and expand. My Father God's Blue Flame of Power enhances the Golden Flame of Eternal Peace and Abundance within the hearts of all Humanity. My Mother God's Pink Flame of Divine Love directs the Flame of Eternal Peace and Abundance through every Heart Flame, and floods the Earth to bless all Life. The Christ's—the Child of God's — Yellow-Gold Flame of Wisdom enlightens every mind to the Divine Truth that Eternal Peace and God's Abundance are inseparable aspects of Divinity. And all is well.

I realize these are days of great acceleration due to the influx of Divine Consciousness that is now flooding the Earth. The vibratory action of every facet of Life is being stepped up the maximum that Cosmic Law will allow in every 24-hour period. The Golden Flame of Eternal Peace and God's Abundance now pouring through my heart, assists me in maintaining balance through this process.

I AM my I AM Presence, and my Father-Mother God are able to easily move through me. My eyes become blazing rays of Light through which the Light of God blesses all Life. My hands become mighty conductors of God's Healing Power. My lips become the instruments through which God's words are formed and directed into the physical plane of Earth. My feet walk the Path of Light. My Lifeforce now becomes the vehicle through which God enters the world to Love and serve all Life.

I now realize and accept my unlimited ability to do whatever I desire in order to establish and expand God's Perfection in my world and the worlds of all Humanity. Through my thoughts, words, feelings, and actions, I AM a mighty, balancing activity of Light pulsating in, through, and around every electron of Life on Earth.

*I AM my I AM Presence, and I invoke the*
*I AM Presences of all Humanity.*

*As one voice, one heartbeat, one breath, one energy, and vibration of pure Divine Love I affirm:*

*I AM a Golden Sun of God's Eternal Peace and Abundance*
*now made manifest and sustained by Holy Grace.*

*I AM a Golden Sun of God's Eternal Peace and Abundance*
*now made manifest and sustained by Holy Grace.*

*I AM a Golden Sun of God's Eternal Peace and Abundance*
*now made manifest and sustained by Holy Grace.*
*And so it is.*

I AM reclaiming the infinite flow of God's Abundance. The perfection of the New Earth is becoming a tangible reality in my life.

I AM One with all Life. I AM a surrogate for Humanity. God's Abundance and Eternal Peace are restored in my life and the lives of every awakening soul.

I AM manifesting my financial freedom and the God supply of all good things. This is providing the necessary sustenance and support I need to fulfill my Divine Plan.

Through the eyes of my I AM Presence, I clearly see that God's Abundance *is* my Birthright. As I assimilate this Truth, the Divine Intelligence blazing in my heart exposes the fact that all of the beliefs I have ever had that were based in poverty, lack, and limitation were merely illusions.

The supply of all good things, financial freedom, opulence, and abundance are God's gifts to me and to all of the Sons and Daughters of God evolving on Earth. Prosperity consciousness floods into my mind and heart, and I see new innovative ways to create prosperity in my life.

Through my I AM Presence, I graciously accept and expect the infinite flow of God's Abundance in my life, now and forever. I know the ebb and flow, the Inbreath and Outbreath, of my Lifeforce is a Universal Law; so in return for my gift of Life, I willingly and joyously agree to share my abundance with those who are striving to cocreate the New Earth. This is my gift of Love, which I AM giving back to God in appreciation for my gift of Life... *as I give, so shall I receive.*

I AM at peace with the concept of sharing my money and my abundance with others, knowing full well that God's Abundance is limitless. The fear of scarcity from my human ego no longer manipulates me. My I AM Presence is in control, and I know that by continually sharing my money and my gifts of abundance with those who are working to fulfill the Divine Plan, I open the door for a perpetual flow of abundance into my own life. This is a Universal Law of Life. It is the Law of the Circle.

The Golden Light of Eternal Peace and God's Abundance is now blazing through every particle of Life as it bathes the physical, etheric, mental, and emotional strata of Earth. This activity is forming a powerful catalyst of God's Abundance which is empowering awakening Humanity to joyfully accept our financial freedom.

On behalf of all Humanity, I AM completely open and receptive to God's Abundance, and I freely give and joyously receive my wealth. I AM therefore, eternally blessed with financial freedom, opulence, abundance, and the God supply of ALL good things. Through my newfound prosperity consciousness, all of the financial sustenance I need to fulfill my Divine Plan is now flowing into my life daily and hourly.

I accept and know that through the full-gathered momentum of the I AM Presence pulsating in every heart, this glorious activity of Light is expanding in power and might daily and hourly with every breath I take. Through the Grace of God, it is Victoriously Accomplished.

I now know and accept, *"the Light of God is ALWAYS Victorious, and I AM that Light."*

And so it is!

# CHAPTER TWELVE

# THE DAY OF THE SEVENTH ANGEL

The Seventh Angel is sounding his mighty Trumpet. He is heralding the New Age of Aquarius. Since the latter part of the 1800's, we have been experiencing the building momentum of the Dawn of the Aquarian Age. Now we have officially entered the full embrace of the forcefield of Aquarius. The Beings of Light have confirmed that in February 2009, we experienced the specific celestial alignments that we were told would mark our official entrance into the Age of Aquarius. Spiritual astrologers have confirmed that this specific alignment did not occur for 1000 years before or 1000 years after the alignments that took place in February 2009.

Our official entrance into the forcefield of Aquarius opened a portal that allowed the greatest influx of the 5th-Dimensional frequencies of the Violet Flame that Humanity has ever been able to receive. The Seventh Angel is now sounding his Cosmic Tones throughout the Universe, and the mystery of God is being fulfilled.

The predominant influence for all Life on Earth during the next 2000-year cycle will be the Seventh Solar Aspect of Deity. This Sacred Fire is the Violet Flame of God's Infinite Perfection, which reflects the perfect balance of the polarities of our Father-Mother God. It also reverberates with the Divine Qualities of Physical Perfection, Mercy, Compassion, Forgiveness, Transmutation, Freedom, Liberty, Divine Justice, the Power of Invocation, Opportunity, Divine Ceremony, and Victory.

It is because of the astronomical power and might contained within the frequencies of this Violet Flame that Jesus knew, in the Day of the Seventh Angel, we would at long last understand his message and regain Christ Consciousness. This is what Jesus was referring to when he spoke of the *Second Coming of the Christ,* and the mystery of God being fulfilled. He was proclaiming the time when Humanity en masse would return to Christ Consciousness and reclaim our Divine Birthright as Beloved Children of God. Jesus also said that *"In the Day of the Seventh Angel, time will be no more."* This is because we are Ascending into the timeless, spaceless frequencies of the 5th Dimension.

For the very first time on this planet, this Age is being referred to as the *Permanent Golden Age*. We have experienced Golden Ages in the past, but they were not permanent. The reason is that during those Ages very illumined souls would embody on Earth, and through their Light they would be able to lift up all who were in their spheres of influence. As long as these souls were in embodiment, the Golden Ages flourished. When it was time for those souls to leave the physical plane, however, their forcefield of Light was removed from the planet with them. Without the support of their Light, the souls left behind could not sustain the Golden Age. This is similar to what happened to the Disciples after Jesus' Ascension.

That is not going to happen during this Golden Age. This time there is not going to be one Avatar or illumined soul who comes into embodiment and lifts up everyone in his or her sphere of influence. This time every man, woman, and child on Earth is going to heal our self-inflicted separation from our Father-Mother God. We are going to regain Christ Consciousness through our own endeavors. We are going to once again become the empowered Children of God, the Christ grown to full stature, which our Father-Mother God intended from our inception.

Once this Golden Age is established on Earth in all of its splendor, there is not going to be one person who will leave the planet and take enough Light to cause the end of the Golden Age. This time when one person leaves and withdraws his or her Light, there will be billions of Lightworkers left behind to sustain the Golden Age.

We are cocreating this reality. As we awaken and remember who we are and why we are on Earth at this time, we are beginning to join together to cocreate the wonders of Heaven on Earth. This is what we agreed to do when we were blessed with embodiment on this planet during this unprecedented experiment. This is what our I AM Presences and the entire Company of Heaven are ready to assist all of us to accomplish, right here and right now. All we have to do is ask.

There is not a more powerful way to transmute the surfacing negativity or to establish the patterns of perfection for the New Earth than the unfathomable gift of the Violet Flame of God's Infinite Perfection. The following information and invocations have been given to Humanity by the Company of Heaven to inspire us and to motivate us into action. The more we utilize these gifts and invoke the Violet Flame, the sooner we will reach a critical mass and tangibly experience the transformation of our lives both individually and collectively as a global family. Listen to your heart, and be the powerful force of Light you have volunteered to be during this Cosmic Moment on Earth.

## THE VIOLET FLAME

The Violet Flame of God's Infinite Perfection is a gift of balanced Light from our Father-Mother God. The Divine Intent of this gift is to help Humanity transmute the human miscreations we have deliberately or inadvertently manifested through the misuse of our thoughts, feelings, words, and actions. This includes anything that exists in the physical plane that is not reflecting the love, harmony, and balance of Heaven on Earth. The Violet Flame is the perfect balance of the Outbreath of our Father God, the sapphire blue Flame of Divine Will, Power and Authority, and the

Inbreath of our Mother God, the crystalline pink Flame of Trans-figuring Divine Love, Adoration and Reverence for Life.

When the Outbreath and the Inbreath of our God Parents merge into one rhythmic pulsation, a Violet Flame of unfathomable power and might is birthed into existence. This sacred gift of Violet Fire has the ability to transmute into Light every malady existing on Earth and every electron of energy Humanity has ever misqualified. I know from the consciousness of our finite minds that seems too good to be true, but the reality is that statement does not even begin to reveal the incomparable assistance contained within this gift from our Father-Mother God.

Ascended Master Saint Germain has been instrumental in bringing the knowledge of the Violet Flame to the conscious minds of Humanity. In the Heavenly Realms, he is known as the Son of Freedom, and he has volunteered to sustain the Violet Flame on Earth for the benefit of all Life evolving here. In his exalted service in the Heart of our omniscient, omnipresent, omnipotent Father-Mother God—All That Is—he is the Keeper of the Violet Flame. In this octave of Divine Service, Saint Germain sustains this gift from our Father-Mother God for all of the Sons and Daughters of God throughout the Universe.

During this critical time on Planet Earth, Saint Germain is working with the support of the entire Company of Heaven. Every Adept, Avatar, Buddha, Saint, and Christed Being who has ever walked the Earth is helping Saint Germain in his endeavor to assist Mother Earth and all Life evolving upon her to Ascend into the 5th-Dimensional frequencies of infinite physical perfection.

In addition to this Divine Intervention, the Legions of Light from Suns beyond Suns and Galaxies beyond Galaxies throughout the whole of Creation are focusing their Love and assistance on this blessed planet. Never have the Children of God received as much help from On High as we are receiving during this Cosmic Moment. Now it is time for us to give something back to the Universe in appreciation for the overwhelming gift of Love that is being rendered to each of us.

In 1936, Saint Germain began revealing information about the Violet Flame to awakening Humanity. At that time, even the Lightworkers were able to withstand only the most gentle frequencies of this Sacred Fire. Saint Germain started by teaching Lightworkers how to use the Violet Flame's gentle qualities of mercy, compassion, and forgiveness. As time progressed, Lightworkers learned to use the frequencies of transmutation and purification. Eventually the Violet Flame frequencies of justice, liberty, freedom, opportunity, and victory became known to us. As we developed the ability to withstand greater Light, we learned how to use the rhythm and Divine Ceremony of the Violet Flame.

The more proficient Lightworkers became in utilizing the gifts of the Violet Flame, the more Saint Germain and the Beings of Light associated with this Sacred Fire were able to help the masses of Humanity lift above our humanly created effluvia. This effluvia was the shroud of darkness that disconnected us from our I AM Presences and prevented us from communicating with the Beings of Light in the Realms of Illumined Truth. For over *seven decades,* Lightworkers around the world have been invoking the Violet Flame, slowly and steadily clearing the way for the awakening that is now taking place within the hearts and minds of people everywhere.

During this vitally important time on Planet Earth, Saint Germain and the Legions of Light associated with this gift from our Father-Mother God are offering to be the open door for an unprecedented 5th-Dimensional frequency of the Violet Flame that will greatly assist Humanity in our Ascension process.

Due to the incredible changes that have successfully taken place within Humanity's Earthly bodies over the past several years and the influx of Divine Consciousness that is bathing Humanity daily and hourly, we are capable of assimilating higher frequencies of the Violet Flame than ever before. Our Father-Mother God have assured us that the Violet Flame will now expand exponentially with every invocation we make, which will help us to quickly transmute the negativity that is being pushed to the surface to be healed, both in our individual lives and around the globe.

This greatly empowered 5th-Dimensional frequency of the Violet Flame will accelerate the awakening taking place on the planet and catapult Humanity up the Spiral of Evolution into frequencies of harmony and balance beyond anything we have experienced since our fall from Grace millions of years ago. This selfless act of Divine Intervention by Saint Germain and his fellow exponents of the Violet Flame will assist Humanity in ways beyond the comprehension of our finite minds. To get an inkling of what this will mean in our everyday lives, we need to understand just how the Violet Flame works.

## HOW THE VIOLET FLAME WORKS

The Violet Flame is available to every man, woman and child evolving on Earth. All we have to do to take advantage of this amazing gift from our Father-Mother God is invoke it into our lives through our I AM Presence. Like all assistance from the Heavenly Realms, we must ask before we can receive. This amazing tool will not interfere with our free will, but once we ask for the Violet Flame to intervene in our Earthly experiences, the floodgates of Heaven open, and the Violet Flame will follow our decree and accomplish whatever we ask it to do.

When we invoke the Violet Flame through our I AM Presence, we give permission for this Sacred Fire to enter our lives. The Violet Flame flows through our Silver Cord into our Crown Chakra, then it descends into our Immortal Victorious Threefold Flame. When the Violet Fire enters our Heart Flame, it is stamped with our individual electronic pattern. After that is accomplished, it awaits direction from our I AM Presence in order to fulfill its mission.

For example, if we are interested in transmuting the obsolete patterns of poverty consciousness that we developed over many lifetimes through our belief in lack and limitation, we simply ask the Violet Flame to accomplish that goal. This can be done through an invocation. For example:

*"I AM my I AM Presence, invoking the full power of the Violet Flame to transmute the cause, core, effect, record, and memory of every thought, feeling, word, or action I have ever expressed in any time frame or dimension that reflects poverty consciousness or lack and limitation of any kind."*

With that invocation, the Violet Flame immediately goes into action. It blazes forth from our Heart Flame, stamped with our electronic pattern. It travels through the atmosphere of Earth and expands out into the Universe. On its journey, it seeks out and magnetizes to itself every electron of energy vibrating with a frequency of poverty, lack, or limitation that is stamped with our electronic pattern.

No matter how dense the frequency of poverty is that cloaks the energy we misqualified during our many lifetimes, there is still a core of purity in every electron that contains its original Divine Potential. This means that within every electron manifesting as poverty there is still, pulsating within its core, the Divine Potential of God's Infinite Abundance. Within every electron manifesting as hatred, there is still the Divine Potential of God's Infinite Love.

Within every electron of war, there is still the Divine Potential of Eternal Peace. Within every electron of disease, there is still the Divine Potential of Vibrant Health.

Once the Violet Flame engulfs the misqualified energy that is stamped with our electronic pattern, it penetrates into the core of purity in each electron and activates the Divine Potential that is encoded there. As the Divine Potential of God's Infinite Abundance is activated within every electron of our poverty consciousness, the atomic and subatomic particles and waves within the electrons begin to spin more rapidly on their axis. The centrifugal force of this acceleration casts the dark frequencies of poverty, lack, and limitation into the Violet Flame. The Violet Fire instantly consumes the frequencies of poverty and transmutes them back into Light. When the transmuting process feels complete, we must then ask our I AM Presence to fill the void where the frequencies of poverty existed, with the Golden Light of God's Infinite Abundance.

It is important for us to take a minute to grasp the magnitude of what this merciful gift from our Father-Mother God means in our lives. With the consistent use of the Violet Flame, we can actually transmute our negative thoughts, feelings, words, and actions from all of our previous embodiments *before* the Law of the Circle returns them to us, bringing all kinds of problems into our lives. The Violet Flame is truly a gift of Divine Grace that is designed to help us quickly reach a critical mass, so that we will transmute thousands of lifetimes worth of our misqualified energy, *in the twinkling of an eye*.

The Violet Flame can transmute anything we want to heal or transform in our individual lives or on the planet. It can transmute back into Light anything that is not reflecting the love, harmony, and balance of Heaven on Earth. All we have to do is invoke the Violet Flame into action through our I AM Presence, and utilize this gift until we reach a critical mass of whatever it is we want to cocreate.

When invoking the Violet Flame, we can work on specific issues in our lives or tackle global problems. We can also create an invocation that covers the gamut of problems manifesting on Earth. In that case, we can use the invocation as a mantra and be an instrument of the Violet Flame at any time and in any place. For example, a simple invocation might be:

*"I AM my I AM Presence, invoking the full power of the Violet Flame to transmute the cause, core, effect, record, and memory of every thought, feeling, word, or action Humanity has ever expressed in any time frame or dimension that reflects anything less than the infinite perfection of God."*

By memorizing a simple affirmation like this, we can say it frequently throughout the day. Then we will be a constant force of the Violet Flame wherever we are and whatever we are doing.

Occasionally, people invoke the Violet Flame without seeing the results in the outer world that they would like to see. This gives them the impression that the Violet Flame is not working, but that is never the case. The Violet Flame is a gift of Divine Light that works scientifically to the letter each and every time it is invoked by the I AM Presence. Remember our discussion about reaching a critical mass. Keep on keeping on! Know that the Light of God is ALWAYS Victorious, and YOU are that Light.

# INVOKING THE VIOLET FLAME

*Through the Presence of God, I AM, now blazing in my heart, I invoke ALL of the Legions of Light who are associated with the 5th-Dimensional frequencies of the Violet Flame.*

*On behalf of myself and ALL Humanity, I AM now blazing the 5th-Dimensional frequencies of the Violet Flame through every atomic and subatomic particle and wave of Life on Earth that is vibrating at a frequency less than the harmony and balance of God.*

*Beloved I AM, look into my life and the lives of ALL Humanity and see what yet remains to be balanced by us to any person, place, condition, or thing we may have wronged at any time, in any way, for any reason.*

*Reach your great, loving hands of Light into all of the positively qualified energy we have released throughout our Earthly sojourns, and draw forth a thousand times as much perfection as we have ever done wrong.*

*Fashion from this substance of perfection a gift of Love, whatever is necessary to balance every debt we have created which still remains unpaid to any part of Life.*

*Beloved I AM, I ask you to forgive every person, place, condition or thing which may have wronged us in any way, and balance all debts owed to us by Life everywhere. I accept this done through the Power of God I AM.*

*And so it is.*

# THE VIOLET FLAME OF 1,000 SUNS

I now invoke Saint Germain and the Mighty Guardians and Cosmic Beings who are associated with the Violet Flame of God's Infinite Perfection. Blessed Ones, come now, and blaze forth the most powerful cleansing activity of this Sacred Fire that Humanity and the Earth are capable of receiving during this Cosmic Moment.

I open my Heart Chakra, and I AM instantly the open door for the most powerful 5th-Dimensional frequencies of the Violet Flame of God's Infinite Perfection the Earth has ever experienced.

The Violet Flame blazes through my heart and expands in, through, and around all inharmonious actions, all lower human consciousness, and all obstructions of the Light that any person, place, condition, or thing has ever placed in the pathway of Life's perfection. The Violet Flame transmutes this discordant energy, cause, core, effect, record, and memory NOW and FOREVER.

The Legions of the Violet Flame take their strategic positions over every country, state, city, town, village, and hamlet on the planet. They reach out their great loving arms and raise up a limitless number of souls in every location who are willing to participate in the faithful use of the Violet Flame of God's Infinite Perfection.

Each of these Lightworkers understands the full importance of this sacred gift now being offered by our Father-Mother God to help free Humanity from all of our human distresses. The conscious use of this mighty power from the Heart of God is establishing within every one of these places great foci of the Violet Flame, which will continually bathe every person in each vicinity.

Now, through the clarion call of the I AM Presence of ALL

Humanity and the Legions of Light throughout infinity, the Violet Flame begins to expand and expand. It merges with the Immortal Victorious Threefold Flame blazing in every person's heart and explodes into a tremendous Starburst of Light. This influx of the Violet Flame increases to *the intensity and power of a thousand Suns*.

Beloved Legions of Light associated with the Violet Flame of God's Infinite Perfection...

*a)* Blaze the Light of a thousand Suns through the thoughts, words, actions, and feelings of every man, woman, and child evolving on Earth until every person individually acknowledges and accepts the Immaculate Concept, the Divine Blueprint, for every facet of Life. Increase this activity of Light daily and hourly until every person's thoughts, feelings, words, and actions are a healing benediction.

*b)* Blaze the Light of a thousand Suns through all incoming babies, the children, their parents, and guardians until ALL youth are raised up in energy, vibration, and consciousness to carry out the directives of their I AM Presences.

*c)* Blaze the Light of a thousand Suns through all youth centers and activities; all schools, colleges, and universities; all leaders, teachers, instructors, and professors in every line of endeavor; until the Flame of God Illumination and Enlightenment is manifest and eternally sustained within every person's heart and mind.

*d)* Blaze the Light of a thousand Suns through all religious and spiritual teachings, so that Divine Love, Truth, Tolerance, and Universal Sisterhood and Brotherhood will quickly manifest.

*e)* Blaze the Light of a thousand Suns through all doctors, nurses, healers, hospitals, insurance companies, pharmaceutical conglomerates, and every institution associated with healing of any kind until Divine Mercy, Compassion, Healing, and Vibrant Health are tangible realities for every evolving soul.

*f)* Blaze the Light of a thousand Suns through all banking and financial institutions; all economic systems; all money and the people associated with monetary interactions of any kind until every person on Earth is openly demonstrating true integrity, honesty, generosity, fairness, abundance, and the God supply of all good things.

*g)* Blaze the Light of a thousand Suns through all places of incarceration and all employed there; through every correctional institution; and every judge, jury and court of law until Divine Justice is manifest and eternally sustained.

*h)* Blaze the Light of a thousand Suns through all space activities throughout the world until every nation unites in cooperative service, so that God's Will may be manifest with our sisters and brothers throughout the Universe.

*i)* Blaze the Light of a thousand Suns through the Heart Flame of every person associated in any way with the governments or the military on this planet. Clear the way for the I AM Presence of each one to take control and to reveal the path of Eternal Peace, God's Abundance, Divine Love, and Reverence for Life.

*j)* Blaze the Light of a thousand Suns through the physical, etheric, mental, and emotional bodies of Humanity until all disease, aging, and human miscreations, their cause and core, are dissolved and transmuted into purity, vibrant health, eternal youth, and physical perfection.

*k)* Blaze the Light of a thousand Suns through the entire Elemental Kingdom serving Humanity and the Earth until all pollution is transmuted into Light and the Immaculate Concept of the New Earth is physically manifest.

*l)* Blaze the Light of a thousand Suns through the food and water industries and through all of the food and water used for human consumption until every particle of food and every molecule of water is filled with Light. Empower this Elemental substance to raise the vibratory action of Humanity's physical, etheric, mental, and emotional bodies until physical perfection becomes a sustained manifest reality for every Human Being.

*m)* Blaze the Light of a thousand Suns in, through, and around every remaining electron of precious Life energy until the Immaculate Concept of the New Earth is manifest, and all Life evolving here is wholly Ascended and FREE.    And so it is.

## DIVINE  GOVERNMENT  INVOCATION

I AM breathing the Breath of the Holy Spirit into the deepest recesses of my Being. Every breath I take cleanses my physical, etheric, mental, and emotional bodies. I hold the focus of my attention on each breath as it lifts me into the embrace of my I AM Presence.

*I AM a Child of God, and ALL that my*
*Father-Mother God have is mine.*
*Father-Mother God, come now and assert your*
*rightful authority within me and ALL Humanity.*

*Help us to cocreate the patterns of perfection for the*
*governments of the New Earth. These governments*
*are based in Reverence for all Life,*
*and the highest good for all concerned.*

*They are governments:*
*OF the I AM Presences of Humanity,*
*BY the I AM Presences of Humanity,*
*FOR the I AM Presences of Humanity.*

In the full power and authority of the Presence of God, I AM, we, the Children of Earth, Ascend into the Heart of our Father-Mother God. From this focus of Light, we invoke into the physical plane of Earth the most intensified Blue Flame of God's Will ever manifested in the history of time.

We ask the Legions of Light serving this blessed Earth to absorb the Flame of God's Will into their Beings and to project this Sacred Fire into the Heart Flame and the conscious mind of every person associated with the governments of this planet at national, state, and local levels.

Blaze the Cosmic Flame of God's Will through each of these souls, and clear away any destructive activity of their own free will which might rush in to try and impede their conscious desire to do God's Will.

Help them to BE God in action at ALL times. Seal all governmental positions, individually and collectively, in the radiance of God's Will.

Reveal through the Flame of Illumination, the Divine Plan and purpose of each office and each individual, and give to each person the spiritual courage and the desire to fulfill that plan perfectly. Let the Will of God be manifest in, through, and around all the governments of the world— NOW and FOREVER!

Let the LIGHT OF GOD THAT IS ETERNALLY VICTORIOUS illumine and lead ALL Humanity everywhere! We consciously accept this manifesting NOW...even as we call.   And so it is, Beloved I AM.

# CHAPTER THIRTEEN

## 2012

There is a lot of misinformation circulating about what will happen in 2012. Most of it is fear-based and predicting things like cataclysmic earth changes and the end of the world. In Truth, we have already entered the initial impulse of the Shift of the Ages. We began our ascent up the Spiral of Evolution into the 5th Dimension in November 2003. That does not mean, however, that 2012 is not important. It is very significant. Whenever the collective consciousness of Humanity is focused on a particular moment in time, we have a tremendous opportunity to cocreate something together. Depending on what we are focusing on, that cocreation can be either wonderful or devastating. It is important for us to realize that whatever happens in 2012 will be the result of what you and I and every other person on this planet empower with our thoughts, feelings, words, and actions between now and 2012.

Since we have already begun our Ascension into the 5th-Dimensional Realms of God's Infinite Perfection, our ability to quickly manifest the archetypes for the New Earth has been greatly enhanced. We need to pay attention to the negativity that is surfacing to be transmuted back into Light so that we can invoke the Violet Flame and transmute it, but we must not stay stuck there. Once we invoke the Violet Flame, we need to focus our attention on what we want to cocreate on the planet instead of the surfacing negativity.

One of my favorite quotes from Buckminster Fuller is *"In order to change something, we do not try to alter the existing model. We create a new model and make the old one obsolete."* This is what we need to do with the existing systems on Earth that are not working toward the highest good for all Life. For instance, the banking systems and Wall Street have proven that there is no depth of greed or corruption to which they will not sink. Instead of waiting for the people to change who are still being grossly manipulated by their human egos, people with a higher consciousness need to create new monetary systems that will make the old ones irrelevant. Instead of waiting for the corporations who are creating the devastating pollution on the planet to develop a reverence for Life, people with a higher consciousness need to reach up and tap into the viable solutions that are now available in the Causal Body of God.

Our time is at hand! This is our moment! The key is that we need to face these challenges and cocreate new options without falling into the consciousness of *"us against them."* There is no separation. We are One.

Because of the intensity of the challenges Humanity is going through, the Company of Heaven is asking awakened Lightworkers around the world to utilize the collective Cup of Humanity's consciousness between now and 2012. We are being asked to cocreate a forcefield of Transfiguring Divine Love that will envelop the Earth and all Life evolving upon her. This will help shift the mass consciousness of Humanity by revealing the Oneness of ALL Life in new and profound ways. As the Infinite Love of God floods into the hearts and minds of unawakened souls, they will be able to raise their heads above the chaos and confusion in their lives. Then they will remember who they are and why they are here, and the Truth of their Oneness with all Life will be reflected in their behavior patterns.

Go within and ask the Presence of God pulsating in your heart to reveal to you your part in this Divine Plan. If you feel the heart call to participate, please join with fellow Lightworkers from around the world. Weave your radiant Light into the Chalice of this Divine Mission, and offer to serve as a surrogate on behalf of your brothers and sisters in the family of Humanity. Prepare to release the residue of the behavior patterns that no longer serve your highest good, as you pave the way for an unprecedented shift of consciousness.

Every day deliberately use your thoughts, feelings, words, and actions to add to the Light of the world. You have been training for lifetimes to do this. Ask your I AM Presence for guidance. Listen to your heart. Trust yourself. You are powerful beyond your knowing.

## HEALING THE POLARIZATION

Day by day more and more people are awakening. This inspires them to lift their hearts and minds, which, in turn, raises their consciousness and allows the Light of God to increase on Earth. When our consciousness is raised and the Light of God increases in our lives, we begin to *"see with new eyes and hear with new ears."* This phenomenon has the wonderful effect of allowing us to clearly perceive the Oneness of Life and the Divine Truth that all Life is interconnected, interrelated, and interdependent. We then know beyond a shadow of a doubt that we are all One and that there is no such thing as *"us and them."*

When this reality resonates in the deepest recesses of our hearts, the validity of war becomes impossible to accept, and the concepts of poverty, greed, corruption, violence, abuse of power, oppression, hatred, selfishness, prejudice, pollution, disease, ignorance, and every other reflection of our belief in separation become intolerable.

Often, from our newly awakened state of consciousness, our reflex response is to take a stand against these negative situations and behavior patterns. Unfortunately, this causes us to polarize ourselves against the people involved. Any time we polarize ourselves against a person or group of people, we motivate them to fight back. This merely widens the abyss between us and causes further separation. We attempt to solve this problem by arguing our case and trying to coerce the people we are polarized against into seeing things our way. We share all of our newly acquired insights and try to convince them that their way of thinking and feeling are flawed. They, in turn, argue from their perspective that our way of thinking is delusional and that we are being duped by unrealistic idealism. Of course, these arguments are futile and only exacerbate our polarization.

It is time for all of us to really grasp the fact that PEOPLE DO NOT KNOW WHAT THEY DO NOT KNOW. When a person awakens, his or her consciousness is raised up, and their perception of reality is transformed. An awakened person literally thinks, feels, sees, and hears with greater awareness. This shift of consciousness allows the person to perceive a greater Truth and to comprehend the Oneness of Life at a deeper level. This awakening results in an indisputable inner knowing within the person's heart and mind.

When an unawakened person tries to deny or discredit the inner knowing of an awakened person, it is futile. That effort is like a deaf and blind person trying to convince a sighted-hearing person that there is no such thing as color or music. The difference in that situation is that the sighted-hearing person would understand perfectly why the deaf and blind person was having trouble grasping the concept of color and music. The sighted-hearing person would have compassion for the deaf and blind person and would respond to him or her with patience and understanding.

Unfortunately, we cannot easily tell if someone is awakened or not. We often make the mistake of assuming that people should know more than they do, or that they should understand more than they are capable of understanding. When we expect more from people than they are capable of, we are generally disappointed and frustrated with their actions and their perception of things, which only polarizes us further.

This is a very challenging time for people everywhere. It is a time when Humanity is being purged, and the negative behavior patterns of our lower human egos are being pushed to the surface to be healed and transmuted. This is a necessary part of our transformation, and a cleansing that must occur in order for Humanity to complete our Ascension into the 5th Dimension. This purification is happening for each of us individually and for all of us collectively.

It seems as though every time we turn on the news, we see widespread reports of corporate greed, governmental corruption, atrocities of war, gross imbalances in the economic system, and myriad other things that reflect Humanity's fear and a belief in separation. These things have existed for a very long time, but they have not been brought to the attention of the masses as profusely as they are at this time.

During this intense time of cleansing and awakening, people around the world are becoming vastly polarized over every conceivable aspect of life. They are polarized over the wars, the economy, taxes, health, health insurance, the justice system, politics, government, religion, education, family values, life-styles, energy, security, business, management, labor, medicine, food, water, air, the environment, and on and on ad infinitum.

We have been told by the Beings of Light in the Realms of Illumined Truth that Humanity is in the midst of the greatest shift of consciousness ever known. The Earth and all her Life are Ascending up the Spiral of Evolution into the 5th-Dimensional Realms of Infinite Physical Perfection. In order for the Earth and Humanity to complete this Ascension process and for Heaven on Earth to become a manifest reality, we must heal the polarization.

Then God's Eternal Peace and Abundance will be the order of the new day on this planet.

Since unawakened Humanity cannot easily grasp the concept of the Oneness of Life, it is up to awakened Lightworkers to heal the polarization. This means you and me and every other awakened soul on Earth. This is our purpose and reason for being in embodiment at this time, and we already have everything we need within us to accomplish this mighty feat.

What affects one part of Life affects all Life. In other words, as I AM lifted up in consciousness ALL Life is lifted up with me. Instead of polarizing against everything we disagree with, we need to create a new reality, a reality that reflects our Oneness and makes the concept of separation obsolete.

We have the opportunity to assist in this endeavor daily and hourly, as we take the power of our attention away from the illusion of separation and focus it on the vision of Heaven on Earth. When we observe something in our life or in the world that does not reflect Oneness or the Reverence of Life, we can invoke the Light of God into the situation and transmute the negativity associated with it by using the Violet Flame. Then we can envision what we want to create in its place.

Instead of polarizing against our government, for instance, we can invoke the I AM Presences of the people who hold public office and ask them to take command of their thoughts, feelings, words, and actions. Then we can visualize the public officials striving for the highest good for all Humanity. When greed, selfishness, and the gross imbalances in the distribution of wealth are brought to our attention, we can invoke the I AM Presences of the people involved in these activities as well. We can envision their I AM Presences taking command of their hearts and minds, and we can visualize their responding with integrity, generosity, and a willingness to assist those who are less fortunate than themselves.

Whatever we focus our thoughts, words, actions, and feelings on, we bring into form. We need to create the vision of what we want life on Earth to be like, and then we need to set about creating that new reality.

In addition to empowering the vision of Heaven on Earth with our every thought, word, feeling, and action, we have the ability to serve as surrogates on behalf of all Humanity. Since all Life is interconnected, when we lift into a higher level of consciousness or transmute an aspect of our human consciousness that no longer serves our highest good, we also lift and transmute the collective consciousness and energies of all Humanity as well.

As we transmute our own obsolete behavior patterns, we need to simply ask the I AM Presence of every man, woman, and child to lift their consciousness and to transmute their negative behavior patterns simultaneously. The Universal Law is: Ask and you shall receive. Knock and the door will be opened.

In deep gratitude for our ability to serve Life on this sweet Earth, let's join together and cocreate a unified forcefield of Transfiguring Divine Love. This forcefield will be far more powerful in its impact on Humanity's global consciousness than any of the other humanly generated forcefields of energy perpetuating the serious problems facing us on this planet. It is a Universal Law that if the inner conditions or forces within Humanity's global consciousness are transformed through Love, the outer conditions of the world will proceed to reflect the Divine Plan for the Earth.

The Divine Plan for the Earth is a living, active, all-powerful forcefield that will produce perfection if not interfered with by our human egos. In the Heavenly Realms, the Beings of Light work purely and precisely with the great forces of Cause, knowing full well that the effects will take care of themselves. Most of us are currently trying to manage EFFECTS in our lives rather than focusing on the CAUSE which will truly change the situation from within. Trying to change things by focusing on the effects is like trying to change the reflection in the mirror without changing the object that is causing the reflection. It is a futile effort.

To insure the transformation of inner conditions for Humanity and the Earth, let's join together and create a forcefield of Transfiguring Divine Love. Centered within unity consciousness, our collective spiritual ability will empower each of us to accomplish this Divine Plan.

## VISUALIZATION

Please focus on this visualization now with the full power of your attention, knowing that you are joining in one-pointed consciousness with Lightworkers around the world.

We begin by invoking our I AM Presence and the I AM Presence of every man, woman, and child on Earth to take full dominion of our thoughts, feelings, words, and actions.

Our Father-Mother God now expand the Flame of Transfiguring Divine Love blazing in every person's Heart Flame. This expansion of Light creates a tremendous magnetic Heart of Divine Love that envelops the entire Planet Earth.

This blazing Heart of Transfiguring Divine Love draws to itself the energy, vibration, and consciousness of pure Love from every Ascended level of Being in the Universe. This gift of Love flows into our planetary CAUSE and helps us to manifest the perfection of Oneness and Reverence for ALL Life through the hearts and minds of every man, woman, and child on Earth.

Our Father-Mother God send forth a clarion call, and twelve magnificent Solar Archangels of Transfiguring Divine Love respond. These selfless Beings of Light descend into the atmosphere of Earth from the electronic belt around the Great, Great Central Sun. They take their strategic positions around the planet and willingly prepare to assist in this activity of Light.

These Solar Archangels are stationed equal distance around the Earth's equator. As One unified force of Transfiguring Divine Love, they project the Light from their Heart Flames into the center of the Earth. They begin conducting a symphony of Love that ensouls and interpenetrates our Beloved Mother Earth and all Life evolving upon her.

The Love from the Archangels expands through the 5th-Dimensional Solar Heart Chakras of every person on the planet. The I AM Presence of every soul becomes a power point of Light unified in consciousness with the I AM Presence of every other soul. Together we inbreathe, assimilate, expand, and project this forcefield of Transfiguring Divine Love. This Sacred Fire now blazes through all Humanity, the Elemental Kingdom, the Angelic Kingdom, and the entire atmosphere of Earth.

The I AM Presence within every person is the open door for this resplendent Light. At inner levels, every person on the planet is now experiencing this forcefield of Transfiguring Divine Love. Through their I AM Presence, every person is seeing the scintillating colors of Love, smelling the fragrance of Love, and hearing the Cosmic Tones and moving melodies of Love. Through this activity of Light, we are all, truly, Love in action. We are collectively changing the core vibration, the CAUSE, of the primal Light substance, which has gone into the present negative conditions that are surfacing to be healed on Earth.

Through the Love of our Father-Mother God, the Solar Archangels, and our I AM Presence, we are the CAUSE of this magnetic forcefield of Transfiguring Divine Love now anchored on Earth. Together we have set in place the basic, spiritual forces of Transfiguring Divine Love over which Humanity is Ascending out of our long exile in darkness into the 5th-Dimensional Realms of Light.

Unified in consciousness with the Kingdoms of Earth and the Realms of Heaven, we are the open door that no one can shut. We are exploring and rediscovering the Company of Heaven and the Divinity within every person, in which we now find complete support for the fulfillment of our Divine Plans.

This is what our Father-Mother God's magnetic forcefield of Transfiguring Divine Love is attracting to each of us personally and collectively as we live within it. We are being raised into a profound awakening of Supreme Love Consciousness. We are, here and now, the masters of Love we were always destined to be.

We now know ourselves as Beings of Love, accepting responsibility for Loving this sweet Earth and all her Life FREE. We are One with this blessed planet, and the planet is One with us.

The twelve Solar Archangels are now expanding their Light to embrace every Human Being in a Cosmic Forcefield of Transfiguring Divine Love. This forcefield surrounds each of us and is anchored directly within the Divinity of our hearts.

Every person's I AM Presence now affirms with a deep inner knowing:

*I AM a planetary forcefield of Transfiguring Divine Love. The Love of God is now thriving on Earth through me. The Heart of Transfiguring Divine Love now enveloping the Earth is transforming the primal Light substance of my four Earthly Bodies, as well as the physical, etheric, mental, and emotional strata of Earth.*

*I AM changing the inner conditions for the entire planet, and I AM setting this Earth on a new planetary course of Divine Love. I feel complete unity with ALL Life, and now with every Holy Breath I take, I inbreathe, assimilate, expand, and project the Love of God into every aspect of Humanity's day-to-day functioning.*

*I feel this forcefield of Divine Love permanently secured within my Heart Flame and the Heart Flames of ALL Humanity.*

*I accept that this forcefield of Transfiguring Divine Love is manifest now, and forever sustained through God's Holy Grace. It is done, and so it is. Beloved I AM.*

## WHAT SHOULD WE ANTICIPATE?

Even though we have already begun our Ascension into the 5th Dimension, Humanity's focus on 2012 is opening a multidimensional doorway into the Divine Heart and Mind of God. This is creating a moment in time when the focused attention and positive expectations of millions of people around the world have the potential of catapulting this planet and all her Life forward in the Light.

People everywhere are becoming aware of 2012, and anticipation abounds. People are asking, What will happen? How will this personally affect my family and me? Will this event change who I am or how I live? Will it result in peace and abundance in the world? Will there be cataclysmic earth changes? Will it change the way people think and feel about each other? What will this event actually mean in the overall scheme of things on Planet Earth?

As usual, there is a plethora of speculation. People are predicting everything ranging from the instant manifestation of Heaven on Earth to the catastrophic end of the world. The Truth is, Humanity is cocreating this event and not even our Father-Mother God or the Company of Heaven know exactly how the events of 2012 will physically manifest on Earth. The outcome will be determined by Humanity and how we choose to use our free will and our creative faculties of thought and feeling to manifest the patterns of perfection for the New Earth.

One thing is assured, however. Because of the awakening of millions of Lightworkers, this monumental influx of Light will have ONLY POSITIVE RESULTS. The events of 2012 are being orchestrated through the unified efforts of both Heaven and Earth with the intent of accelerating Humanity's awakening process and Earth's Ascension into the 5th Dimension.

The important thing for Humanity to remember is that we are ALL Sons and Daughters of God, and it is our Divine Birthright, our responsibility, and our obligation to cocreate Heaven on Earth in this physical reality. We are the ones who will determine the results of the incredible influx of Light that will take place in 2012.

In order for us to fully understand how this event will affect us personally and collectively, we must remember that we are all multidimensional Beings, and we function in various dimensions of existence simultaneously. This is true even though, on a conscious level, we are usually unaware of anything but the dense physical plane.

Normally, we judge everything by what we perceive to be happening in the outer world. The problem with that is that the physical plane of Earth is the most illusive and the least real of all the dimensions we abide in. It is also the very last dimension to reflect the changes that take place in the Realms of Cause. Our perceptions and our interpretations of what is really going on, based on what we see in the outer world, are usually very distorted and many times totally inaccurate.

When major events such as 2012 take place, the changes occur first and foremost in the Realms of Cause. Then our I AM Presence assimilates the newly formed patterns of perfection and gently projects them into the Threefold Flame in our heart. From our Threefold Flame the changes and all of the Divine Potential associated with them gradually reflect into our conscious mind. We then have the ability to cocreate the new patterns in the world of effects by projecting them into the physical plane through our thoughts, words, feelings, and actions.

If we choose to participate in this process, the patterns become part of our new reality, and we joyously experience them as they manifest in our daily lives. This motivates us to keep on keeping on, and day by day our lives are transformed into expressions of harmony, abundance, happiness, and peace. This process takes place for every person on the planet each time changes of this nature occur in the Realms of Cause, but they unfold in Divine Timing for each person, so no two people are on the same time frame. That is why these events never result in instantaneous global transformation. Instead, they unfold gradually according to each person's Divine Plan, each person's conscious participation in the process, and each person's willingness to be the open door through which the Light of God will flow to cocreate the new patterns of perfection on Earth.

It is important for us not to let our unrealistic expectations determine what we perceive to be the success or failure of 2012. The only things we have experienced in this lifetime that even remotely compare to this impending event are Harmonic Convergence, which took place August 15-17, 1987, and Harmonic Concordance, which took place November 8-24, 2003. During those events, people all over the world were expecting all sorts of miraculous changes too. When people woke up the day after the events, and things seemed pretty much the same, many people lost faith and classified the events as New Age hoaxes. In reality, nothing could be further from the Truth.

Harmonic Convergence and Harmonic Concordance resulted in the greatest influxes of Light the Earth had experienced up to that point. Harmonic Convergence paved the way for Earth's Ascension off of the Wheel of Karma and back onto the Spiral of Evolution. It reactivated Earth's Crystal Grid System and created the environment for the activation of Humanity's twelvefold 4th-Dimensional Solar Spines. Harmonic Convergence began our ascent into the 4th Dimension.

Harmonic Concordance was the initial impulse of the Shift of the Ages, which began the Earth's Ascension into the 5th-Dimensional Realms of God's Infinite Perfection. This shift also began the process of Humanity's transformation from carbon-based Beings into crystalline-based Solar Light Beings. The Light that poured into the planet during these two events awakened a full range of capacities within Humanity, and moved us a quantum leap toward the global awakening we are experiencing now.

If you have any doubts about that, just observe your own growth following these two events. Look at how you matured spiritually, and how your feelings, thoughts, and life have changed since 1987. Then pay attention to the shift that has taken place within your thoughts and feelings since 2003. Observe how many awakened people you know now compared to the number you knew back then. Pay attention to how your own direction has changed since that time, and see how you have moved closer to the fulfillment of your Divine Plan, your purpose and reason for being.

2012 has the potential to be more powerful and more life-changing than Harmonic Convergence or Harmonic Concordance. This is true because of the acceleration of time, and because there are millions more people awake now than there were in 1987 and 2003. This upcoming shift will manifest much more quickly than the changes that took place after Harmonic Convergence or Harmonic Concordance.

With that knowing, ask your I AM Presence and the entire Company of Heaven to guide you carefully, step by step through this process, so you will be the most effective instrument of God you are capable of being during this unique opportunity. Together, we will change the world.

During the time leading up to, including, and following 2012, allow your thoughts and feelings to be filled with an alertness, enthusiasm, and a Divine Intelligence that is forever open and pliable. Do not allow your thinking to become stagnant, or obsolete. The changes that will occur between now and 2012 will lead Humanity to deep and previously unknown possibilities within the human mind. Know that your heart and mind are continual miracles of advancement and spiritual development.

Stay focused on the present and celebrate your every breath, thought, feeling, word, and action. Live your visions, and empower them with love and a deep reverence for Life. From the consciousness of your I AM Presence, live each moment as you desire the future to be, and know that the future will fulfill your desires.

Through our visions and spiritual desires in the present, we will cocreate the future and release the shadows of the past. Our desires and visions of the New Earth will bring astounding results. With courage and faith, we are going to meet this great destiny. Our Divine Purpose will be our every thought, word, and deed. We are embarking on a New Day on this precious planet, and together we are cocreating Heaven on Earth. Stay focused on the Light!

And BE HERE NOW!!

## ABOUT THE AUTHOR

## PATRICIA DIANE COTA-ROBLES

Patricia is cofounder of the nonprofit, educational organization New Age Study of Humanity's Purpose, which sponsors her work and the *Annual World Congress On Illumination.*

Patricia was a marriage and family counselor for 20 years. She now spends her time freely sharing the information she is receiving from the Beings of Light in the Realms of Illumined Truth. This sacred knowledge is designed to give Humanity clarity, understanding, and encouragement as we progress through these wondrous but often challenging times on Earth.

Patricia is an internationally known teacher and has taught workshops in the former Soviet Union, Ireland, England, South Africa, the Dominican Republic, Venezuela, Brazil, Bolivia, Mexico, Canada, Greece, Italy, Australia, New Zealand, Thailand, France, Bali, Turkey, Japan, and throughout the United States of America. She participated in the *Soviet-American Citizens' Summit* in Moscow, and represented the United States in the category of Holistic Models in Health, Psychology, and Healing. Patricia also participated in the *First Global Earth Summit* held in Rio de Janeiro, Brazil. Patricia had the honor of being a presenter at the *"Call to World Peace from the Universal Brotherhood"* gathering in Istanbul, Turkey, and the *"Symphony of Peace Prayers,"* which was a gathering of over 10,000 people that took place at sacred Mt. Fuji in Japan.

Patricia's philosophy is: Every person is precious and Divine, regardless of how far his or her behavior patterns and life experiences may be from reflecting that Truth. We are not the victims of our lives. We are the cocreators of our lives. We have a choice, and we have the ability to transform our lives into what we want them to be. The time for us to do so is now!